Mental Toughness

By

Daniel Anderson

Table of Contents

Introduction.. 6

Chapter 1 9

Mental Toughness 9

Application of mental toughness in science 13

Mental toughness in the Religious circle 16

Chapter 2.. 18

A Psychologist's Guide to Becoming Psychologically
Strong.. 18

Chapter 3.. 29

Develop Resilience 29

What is Resilience 29

Failure is only a Postponed success 31

The ability to receive shock or disappointments........... 32

The secret of being resilient....................................... 37

Study other people who are Resilient 38

Be Patient... 38

Be focus in realizing your dream 39

What does it take to be focused? 40

Learn from the Mistakes of Others 46

Don't give room for Complacency 46

Non-negotiable Fight Back.. 50

How Determination to Succeed causes you to become
resilient 54

Get the required Motivation.. 57

Having a very Strong Ambition 59

Having the Vision 63

Chapter 4.. 66

Self-Discipline & Willpower on Demand..................... 66

Punctuality a Necessity.. 69

Avoid Lateness... 70

Avoid Scandal.. 70
Self Discipline leads to leadership 72
Chapter 5 74
Mindset... 74
Negative Mindset 75
The disadvantages of having a negative mindset 75
Inability to recognize opportunity 76
Passing over opportunities repeatedly 76
How Negative Mindset affects an Individual Mental
Toughness... 77
Negative Mindset leads to procrastination 77
Having a Positive Mindset 78
Believing in yourself... 78
Goal setting.. 79
Write Down Your Goals 79
Chapter 6 81
Mental State... 81
Love and Concentration 82
How Love can affect you negatively........................... 83
Hatred and Mental Toughness 84
Pleasure and Mental toughness 86
Pain and Mental Toughness.. 87
When Pain is caused by Defeat 89
Being Afraid as it Affects Mental Toughness 90
Conceiving Something and Hoping.............................. 91
Chapter 7 92
Develop an Unbeatable Mind...................................... 92
Fearless and Mentally Tough...................................... 93
"Yes I can" - Unbeatable Mindset" 93
Use what you have to your advantage........................... 95
Constant Practice... 96
Be Excited 97

Chapter 8... 100

  Iron Will.. 100

  Being Resolute.. 100

  Don't Accept Excuses... 101

  Having Genuine Integrity 102

  Be Honest.. 103

  Be flexible by Practical...................................... 103

  Be Trustworthy 104

Chapter 8... 105

  Confidence.. 105

  High Self Esteem 105

  Self Believe in Fostering Confidence 106

Chapter 9... 108

  Achieve the Success 108

  Leave your Comfort Zone................................... 108

Chapter 10... 110

  Conclusion 110

Introduction

Mental toughness is a going concern among individuals, organizations and nations. It is a very important subject of great reference and with the constant increase in world population and competition, the existence of stiff competition which cuts across every sector of the world economy and business has made it clear that every person who intends to survive must have to learn the rudiments of being a survivor.

It is interesting to know that long age standing discovery of the term "survival of the fittest has come to prove the existence of a common factor that leads to surviving and that is the "fittest". Now the question you should be asking yourself right now is "am I mentally tough enough to fit into the hard situations in the society?"

Mental toughness therefore is not just a topic, it is something that affects every individual in the world today, if you are tough mentally the chances of your survival in the sophisticated and fast developing world is certain. As the population continues to increase and with limited jobs, how do you intend to survive in this information age?

Now is the time for you to look inward and know how you can really become mentally tough. This book is bringing the best pragmatic ways that will show you what you have been missing and what you have not been doing right. I will open up your eyes to the facts and true reality of the nature of the world and you will see what is actually happening.

Then you will be able to determine where you really belong presently, how you can liberate yourself from where you are and graduate or leap to your choice place in life.

You can actually take your destiny into your own hands and chose where to be and when to be and achieve greater heights, mental toughness associates with certain factors and characteristics that will bring out the very best in you when you decide to make a change.

The issues relating to success can be found in people with mental toughness. Hence, successful people are usually mentally tough, there is something that drives them to become very successful, and one of those factors are related to being mentally tough.

Are you having problems in your life? Have you been looking for a way out of your current situation and you are finding it extremely difficult to realize your dreams? Then this book is actually prepared based on vast experience and research.

It will make you to rediscover yourself and become a champion by right and merit.

Nothing comes easy in life except you are born with a silver spoon, and even as at that, you may lost the riches that you have inherited if you don't have the mental toughness or ready to take control of your life, for many have had the opportunity of inheriting great wealth and they are unable to expand with it or manage it well.

Being mentally tough is for both the young and adults.

So take the opportunity provided here and equip yourself for that challenge that comes your way.

Be a different person, stand out from the crowd, be a leader in your area of life and become the champion that you have always dreamed to become, the time is now. Follow the simple steps to become mentally tough to be a survivor and a victorious person. Enjoy!

Chapter 1

Mental Toughness

Before we go further in this wholesome knowledge about mental toughness, let us visualize what we mean by being mentally tough. Hence, what is mental toughness?

Mental Toughness is an evaluation of a person or an individual's ability to become resilient and being confidence that permeates the very cradle of success and actually becoming a success in any life's endeavors such as, education, sports, workplace, career, business, technology, information, science, etc.

As a wide concepts the emergence of various activities in the world brought about mental toughness especially in sports, career, education, business etc. the concepts also starts during the period of training of an individual to become a better person among pairs or groups or as a student who is undergoing some form of training.

However, it is worthy of note that the definition of Mental toughness may vary from the different points of view from different professionals who are in the area of business, sports, science, politics, education etc. but they all have one thing in common and that is an individual must be involved in mental toughness.

Application of Mental toughness in sports;

From the Sports psychologist point of view, they see mental toughness from an athlete point of view, that the athletes needs mental toughness to go through the various rigorous training schedule, to be able to compete with other athletes and to develop his or her ability to have an edge over his opponents.

The sports psychologist believes that the onus is on the athlete to maintain a top level to have the urge and hunger to succeed at every point in time, the athlete must also believe that he or she is capable of making it happen. The sports psychologist wants the athlete to always have a winning mentality and believe that he or she has an edge over other athletes. The responsibility to win must always reverberate in the mind of the athlete especially during competitions.

In the recent years, we have seen many teams in the world of sports employing the services of a sports psychologist, why? Because they believe modern athletes now need psychological boost in any competition or in their career while they play for the team.

This is true as various individuals in the world of sports who are elite athletes doing far better than their contemporaries. Some of the attributes of the elite athlete which makes them better than others are simply because they discovered themselves and they continue to develop themselves to rediscover themselves, they spend more time practicing on their trade and always maintain a high level of discipline, they always make sure that they stay away from scandals, they always make efforts to manage their activities and maximize their biggest potentials.

The winning mentality does not change in them and they always want more, they don't usually give room for complacency and they take each game seriously and always remain focused. These are the various attributes that differentiates the ordinary athlete from the elite and of course these activities always comes with great rewards.

Mental toughness in the education sector

The educational sector is not left out in mental toughness. As you can see in various school curriculums, schools have lined out various subjects including regular assignments that will make the students to read and make sure they are able to carry out assignments and also keep them busy. Any student who is unable to cope with these activities will likely not do well when it comes to education. But if they should discover themselves through other means, such as sports, talents in other areas of life, then they can actually measure up or supersede their contemporaries.

Being the best students sometimes doesn't mean you will make more money more than others or become successful more than others, Bill Gates for example is not a professor but of course he is by far richer than millions of professors in the world. Mark Zuckernberg the owner of facebook doesn't have any manufacturing industry but with facebook he is among the top 5 billionaires that we have in the world today.

Hence, is all about discovering your potential and develop your mental toughness to achieve your dreams.

We have individuals in the world today who have been able to do exploits and are actually ahead of their pairs simply because they have develop the mental toughness, many of them just discovered themselves and are still rediscovering themselves because of one thing and that is "mental toughness" for instance, in sports of football, one man stands out and that is Christiano Ronaldo, from his Portuguese club fc Porto to Manchester United and to Real Madrid and now Juventus, he has been doing one thing and that is "continuous training after training, and he has a passion for scoring lots of goals, he has a winning mentality, he doesn't believe there is any other player better than him, even at his prime, he feels he is just starting.

He disciplined the way he eats, he doesn't just eat any enticing food, he eats what will keep him healthy and fit. Of course, we have had other great players who could have been better than him, but the problems they had was inability to stay consistent at what they do for a long time. And that is just the difference between Christiano Ronaldo and others.

Mental toughness therefore is all encompassing, there is no one direction to being mentally tough, you must have to do certain things that others aren't doing, you must have to think the way others aren't thinking and you must have to keep a lifestyle that is alien to others, only when this is done, you will see a change that is akin to successful people, I'll show you the various attributes that will make you stand out among the crowd, your life will never be the same if you practice what I'll show you as you read on.

As a student you are give your subject outline, you already know what to read and study in school, now, it is very common that not all the students usually pass examination, while some pass the exams in flying colors, not all do pass in flying colors, while some are average not all are also average, some get A, B, C, D, E or F, the question is how come some of the student got "A" which is an excellent result, while some fall into other categories, it didn't just happen by chance, ask yourself the question, what did the students who scored "A" do that others did not do. There must be something behind it. After all, all the students got the same curriculum and are doing the same course, so why did that happened.

It all boils down to one thing, and that is mental toughness. The students that score "A" grade really wanted it and they got it, they did what it takes to get it and that is why they got it, if you tried to get it but fall short of it, it means you did not just do as much as they did to achieve it.

But it is actually achievable, study them carefully and do more the next semester to beat them or equal their feet. Again it's still depends on your level of "mental toughness". If you are not mentally tough you will not be able to meet up with their performance.

Application of mental toughness in science

Most scientists stand out in their career than others simply because they have a diehard mentality that is very tough at discovering something new. A scientist who is not interested in discovering something new will always need to depend on what is already existing, but the one who is inspired and spirited will always desire to invent something, he wants something new to give to the world, something that nobody has ever done.

From history, we have seen scientist who gave us what we are still using today, such as, the principle of developing the LED globe and electricity. Michael Faraday the man who discovered electricity based on a particular principle of electricity he found out through personal discovery, Thomas Edison, the man who discovered the electric bulb tried several times and failed but he never gave up and he ended up giving the world one of the greatest discoveries of man which principle is today the basis of LED electric bulb production. Again, one thing that is common among these men was mental strength, if Thomas Edison gave up his idea on electric bulb, then he would never have discovered it. Mental toughness is the ability to consistently stick to what you believe that is going to work based on experimenting when it comes to scientific discovery.

Many scientists continue to experiment on something until they see that it is going to work, if it doesn't work, they keep on trying until finally they get the result. At this level, this is the scientists' mental toughness, the believe in the positive result of the outcome of what they are inventing. We can also borrow the knowledge of the science way of thinking or mentality to develop the area of life which we found is near impossible to achieve, I'll rather believe that it is going to work, and I'll keep working at it until I get it right.

The only thing that makes it not working for now is simply because you have not gotten it right, and the only way you'll ever get it right is when you keep working it and keep on practicing and doing it till you get it right.

The story of Thomas Edison is very interesting, he kept on believing that his invention will work, he never doubted himself, at the point of giving up, he just discovered what was missing and when he did discovered it, the rest is history, he got it right at that moment, the pain and suffering over the failed attempts was forgotten and what he achieve was what no man ever did achieve, today Thomas Edison is one of the renowned scientist for his good works of discovering the electric bulb.

The difference is that these men continued consistently believing that what they are doing will work and it did work. You will not just believe but add what you are doing to what you believe. With the right believe system that 'it is going to work' and actually doing what you believe is what will give you the result not when you don't believe in what you are doing, that will not give you the right result.

Again a man said during the time of Aristotle, the great Greek philosopher, that man cannot fly, Aristotle opined rather that man will fly, he believed in what he said, but many people mocked him and in response they said to him "You ought to know that you are wrong, even the ostrich with wings cannot fly, why should you ever conceive in your mind that man without wings will fly?" and so nobody believe what he said.

But many years later, man is flying from country to country from one continent to the other and from earth to the moon and outer space. Actually those who usually believe have a better mental strength or toughness than others.

Mental toughness also has to do with what you believe, if you believe in something and you develop a passion for it, you work towards achieving it, you will definitely get that thing. For this has been the story of many people in time past.

Mental toughness in the Religious circle

From the religious perspective, an act of believing is always prominent, and I suggest that there is no way you will have mental toughness without believing in what you are doing, because if you want success in any endeavor you will have to believe in what you are doing. In religious believe for instance, if you want something extra ordinary to happen, you must pray for it and also have faith, therefore faith is all about having the belief, confidence that what you are praying for will come to fruition. In other words, your level of faith or belief will determine the outcome of what you are praying for.

In the bible for instance, when Jesus healed the blind man, there is a question he asked which is "do you believe that the son of Man will be able to heal you?" and the blind mind responded "show me and I'll believe" and after he was healed by Jesus, he asked him to go and tell no one about it.

Hence, to belief in something is a precursor to achieving what you are working at or dreaming about, if you are a student and you want to become a medical doctor or a scientist or venture into any other career, the first thing you need to do is to believe that you can actually realize your dreams, after this, every other thing you need to do follows it.

We can also talk about the mental toughness in religion with the issue of the woman with the issue of blood who had been bleeding for twelve years, she only had one conviction based on her faith, and she believed that if she would be able to touch the master's clothes she will be healed. In the midst of the crowd while she attempted to do that, she actually achieved it, and immediately she touched His clothe, Jesus Christ noticed that power had flown out from His body to heal the woman. He actually stopped and asked "who touched me?" His disciples were surprised because they were all in the midst of the crowed anybody could have touched him, so one of the disciples said to him "master it's possible anyone could have touched you in the midst of the crowed" but He responded "no, it was different, as soon as the person touched me, power flew out of me", the woman noticing she was healed, knew she was the one that was being talked about and she quickly submitted herself.

So, if you don't believe you don't have the mental toughness, start believing and you will achieve that high level of mental toughness that will make you to survive in any of your chosen field in life.

Why we have so many average people in the world today is simply because of the level of individual's mental toughness.

I have seen lots of people with great potential and talents to become superstars, but because of low level of mental toughness, they have not been able to forge ahead in life.

Mental toughness therefore is something that is very important and needs urgent attention. Whatever you do as an individual, to be successful with it, you need to become mentally tough.

Chapter 2

A Psychologist's Guide to Becoming Psychologically Strong

From the previous chapter, I brought to your knowledge the meaning of Mental toughness from different point of view and perspective. In this chapter I shall be taking you through a more scientific methodological approach to mental toughness which is practicable and can be applied in everyday life. It is quite easy to achieve, but there are some certain things you will need to do as an individual for you to be able to become more dominant and get the full benefits of being mentally strong or tough.

I always advice people about mental toughness, it's not about you alone, mental toughness also has to do with your ability to discern, self discovery, knowing your strongest points and developing it, knowing your weakness and improving on it and also having an edge against your competitors or contemporaries. It has to do with your will to develop yourself, to go the extra mile in other to fulfill your dreams.

Note that it is possible to read many books that has to do with personal development, but if there is no will or zeal to apply what you have red from the books, you will never make a headway, it is a different thing to read about personal development and it is another thing to applying it.

Sometimes to enable an individual achieve success or dream, it may take the efforts of others in what I call "the collective responsibility for an individual's development".

From this perspective, it takes a teacher or group of teachers who are teaching in a school to prepare students who are going to become successful in their studies, it also takes a business coach to help a person to grow and become successful in business, and that is why you will meet a lot of people who look up to other people as their mentor or business partners or advisors.

In sports, you'll also find out that a lot of coaches or managers of teams have specific psychological trainers or advisors who see to the mental strength and development of the team, this will enable the team to believe in their capabilities and play to their highest potentials. The duty of the psychologist is to help build the team or individuals to play to their capability or potentials, to believe they are better than their opponents at all times. In this regard therefore, in whatever you do you need to apply this method of mental development which enables you to grow within the ambient of your potentials gradually and get to the peak of success.

Psychologists developed the most practicable means of achieving success much more easily without having to undergo rigorous activities that will enable you to build on your present natural mental strength. I am sure it is something that you can also follow within your capacity to achieve success.

In this determination, I deploy the most practical approach to what can be obtained successfully, however, I must let you know also that, in all circumstances, it is the level of efforts that you put in that will determine yours success, what am I talking about here? I mean if you want something more than any other person, and you decide to do what it takes to be the best, if your best is actually the best of the best, of course you will definitely win, but if your best isn't the best of the best, then expect someone else who actually worked better at being the best of the best to pick the coveted price.

In a nutshell then, I'll like to ask you some questions which are; do you really think you can go the extra mile at achieving something great? Do you really want to beat everyone who is your fellow competitor? Do you think you can win even when others are competiting with you? What do you think about your level of mental strength presently and in the next coming weeks?

If you can find answers to this questions, then, I believe in you, I belief you can become what you want to be, I believe you are unstoppable, but if I believe in you and you don't believe in yourself, you don't let me down, you let you down. That is simply the basic thing, to believe in yourself is what will propel you to victory, and to believe in yourself is what will make you to become the giant in your field of study.

I have watched the late Michael Jackson during his youthful and adult years, I discovered one thing about him, he doesn't believe there is any of his equal, he just be what he is, he was simply Michael Jackson the entertainer, from his childhood, he knows nothing other than music, he lived the life of an entertainer from childhood, his talent was discovered and developed and the strength of his mental toughness was amazing.

He just doesn't accept failure, he was success epitomize, why? Because he stood by and did what he knew how to do best, he believed so much in it and he became what he truly became in the end he wrote his own history on earth. The music industry will not be complete without his story, Guinness books of records will be incomplete without his name, and international awards will not be complete without his name among the greatest legend of music that ever lived.

How did this man succeed? How did he became a very big super star on earth, it takes a person with the right mental toughness to achieve such a feet, no feebly mental person or weak mental individual can achieve what the people that belong to the mental toughness group can achieve the level of success. This is just the difference.

From the foregoing, you will notice and agree that the major problem we have in the world today as far as human beings are concerned is that people do not have access to psychologist who will be able to take care of the mental toughness, in actual fact many do not know that they have a problem of being not being mentally tough, and that is why we will continue to have people who adore and celebrate famous people who actually have the mental toughness to excel in their chosen careers. Have you ever asked yourself, what is so special about sports men and women, actors and actresses, music artists and other celebrities and famous people, why is it that the media talk so much about them and their lifestyle, why is it that they are making all the money that is very huge in the sector where they have pitched their career?

It all boils down to one thing and that is *"their mental toughness has been exploited to their own advantage"*

I strongly believe that if every individual in the world that we live in are mentally tough, many of them will be successful, I'm not bragging about this, it is what I have practically seen happen in real life. There is nothing that can stop an individual from succeeding in life with the right mental toughness.

Mental toughness therefore comes with a price and there are certain characteristics that are usually associated with people who have mental toughness. This will be discussed in subsequent chapters as we read on.

Therefore, if you are reading this book, you should also consider yourself very lucky that you have found the right formula, just like I said, mental toughness is administered to many people who later become famous either they are in a particular field or profession, take for instance, sports men and women who have access to sporting facilities and a psychologist who works on their mental toughness to make sure they maximize their potential, this is the advantage those sports men and women have over ordinary people who are employed in a company.

Many companies don't see the need to get a psychologist to help train the mental toughness of their employees, and so they keep on remaining at the state that they were employed. Although some organizations or companies may decide to carry out regular in-house training, seminar and workshop for their staff, but not all of them do this.

The training by some of these organizations serves as a moral or mental booster. Sometimes the desired results may be achieved but when the employee leaves the employment it just ends there.

The development is more rapid and faster with sports men and women who are always receiving constant training and participate in competitions, they have access to psychologist who is an expert in the field of preparing them ahead of tournaments and club or country engagements. This is what makes the difference, this is what make them to become one of the highest paid or income earners among people. Now this fact has proven that to get a trainer for your mental toughness, you'll need to go the extra mile.

Firstly, if you want to get a psychologist who will help in building your mental toughness, you will need to have the money to afford his services. And if you are unable to pay his or her fee, then you will not get access to a psychologist who will be able to help your situation.

One of the reasons that made me to take a firm decision in writing this book is because I have the interest of people within your category at heart because I really want to help many people rediscover themselves and become mentally tough.

By the time you are finished with the content of this book, you will get big value for your money because, you will be shown what it takes to be mentally tough and as you can see already, you are becoming more in tune with the information in this book.

This book will be a source of reference for anything that has to do with mental toughness, take it up and read while you practice what you read and apply it to your daily life, it is very important to know that, when you get a copy of this book, you can be rest assured that if you cannot pay a psychologist, this book has already done the job for your moral and mental boosting, you will always come back to read the parts that has to do with your mental development as you continue to struggle for survival.

Today, a lot of people need the services of a psychologist, but they would never accept that they do, but in actual fact, the role of a psychologist cannot be overestimated, why because we have seen how they have been able to address so many issues that has to do with individual's underperformances and how they have helped in building them to become great people.

As each individual continue to live daily in the world, we are bound to face many challenges, some of this challenges can only be dealt with if we have the mental toughness, that is why we hear statements like "taking the bull by the horn" everyone will have to face it either we like it or not, there will always be a time when you will need to face reality and you will need to stand up to the test.

If you don't have the mental toughness, you will definitely fizzle out, whether it is business, education, private company or family or even in governance, if you are not mentally tough, don't be surprised you will fizzle out or lost out in the race. If you are in a place of position, someone is watching and planning to take over that position from you, if you are in a position of authority, someone somewhere might just be scheming and planning your downfall so that he or she can take that position from you. It happens all the time.

You have been working in a company for the past five to ten years, you've not gotten any promotion, and someone somewhere is sitting on your promotion. That's how wicked some corporate organization can be, what will you do if you face challenges? Do you feel depressed and give up or you fight and stay strong to claim what is rightfully yours? Whatever you are thinking is still has to do with your mental strength and toughness, if you are weak mentally, there is no way you can survive the maneuvering of some men or women in a business organization who are so desperate for power.

In the circumstances, you will agree with me that every living person in this world needs a psychologist who will help him or her to develop mental toughness, the major reason why people fail to achieve their goal is because they do not have mental toughness, that you fail doesn't mean that you cannot make it in whatever you're trying to achieve. No! is simply because you gave up when you can actually try and improve to achieve that thing. Secondly, there are ways to achieving your goals, a path that needs to be followed, the way that leads to success, is just that you did not follow that path or take the right step in the right direction.

You really need a psychologist's guide if you find it difficult to compete with your contemporaries, life itself is a competition, learning how to survive is possible, but surviving well is very important. Don't just exist without surviving, you may be existing and yet you are not surviving.

For instance, if you have $1,000 in your bank account and a problem of $50,000 comes your way, definitely you are in trouble, because your $1,000 cannot take care of the $50,000 problem. Do you now see?

But if you have a problem of $100,000 and you have $20,000,000 in your bank account, that problem is solved before its starts or ends.

You need to look into yourself and realize why the top earners in the world continue to make more money, while the little income earners, end up spending and not having enough. Is not a mistake, it's simply because the top earners in the world today have develop their mental toughness and tailored it towards achieving success and the results is having more and more income which continues to generate more cash and they are able to invest and earn massively getting to a level of becoming financially free.

These top earners in the world today did not just become superstars over night, it took them sometime, through training and personal development they were able to develop the mindset of staying mentally tough, they became focus and realize what they want and they worked towards it and eventually achieved what they wanted.

The psychologist guide therefore is something that everyone needs, and I will encourage you to always refer back to this book to keep you on the track if you ever encounter any problem, this master piece is the tonic you need to get back on track.

I once met a young man who was feeling depressed, what happened to him was that in his first year in the University, when he got admission, he started attending lectures but found it difficult to follow through or understand the course, some subjects were difficult for him to understand, he approached some of his lecturers, and wanted solution, but only few of them could help, quite a number of them were very busy and wouldn't have the time with him. So he felt dejected and gradually became depressed. His mental status became weak and before he realized it, the exam preparations was very poor and he didn't do well, he failed about four courses out of the twelve and he only managed to pass remaining eight.

While I noticed his countenance, I approached him and he shared his problem with me, I wanted to help him get back on track, I told him something which is what I started with in this book, and that is "to believe" he had lost faith in himself, but I told him I believe he can pass those courses, I told him he can become a better lecturer in those courses he failed, that captivated his attention and he got interested in the conversation, he wanted to know more, because I touched the sensitive part of his mind which is his mental strength, he was still a student, and in that circumstances I had to figure out a way to reach his brains. I said something that triggered his mind and he got the booster he needed, he believed because I believed in him, I believed that he could do it and he got inspired because I believed he could do it.

That moment we chatted turned around to become a moment of change in his life and he got up and thanked me very much, I gave him a lift, I got him back on track when he wondered away, many people in the world are just like that.

Why do you think many people commit suicide? Is no difference, they may find frustration in the "hand of life", they weren't expecting their life will turn out to be what it is now and they give up all hopes, hence, because there is no one to help them back on track, they end up in depression, self pity and the frustration is too much for them to handle, then, the next thing they do is committing suicide. This guide is the basic change mantra that will change your life, change your mindset and develop you into a mentally tough person that you have to be to become that great person you ought to be.

Chapter 3

Develop Resilience

Before I go further to talk about being resilient, I want you to take a deep breath and think within yourself; ask yourself the question about resilience, what does it take to be resilience? Am I resilient? What makes you think that you are resilient?

Let me start by discussing about what it means to be resilience.

What is Resilience

From the definition given by Merriam Webster's collegiate dictionary, Resilience is the capability of a strained body to recover its size and shape after deformation caused by comprehensive stress, secondly, it is an ability to recover from or adjust easily to misfortune or change, being able to recover from shock without being permanently deformed.

One of the major factor that has kept successful and famous people going, is their level of resilience, whether it is sports, business, education, technology and in all sector of life, the one thing that always differentiates successful people from the most hostile business environment or competitive environment is their uncommon mental toughness to succeed, I've seen circumstances when people who are thriving to succeed in a very difficult situation lost their ability to remain resilient despite the difficult situation they are facing, most of them end up giving up on their dreams and they also fizzle out or change environment to some other places. Why is it so, it's simply because they have not fashioned a way of remaining resolute in their quest for survival.

If you must be resilient you must make up your mind not to give up on difficult situations, you must stand firm no matter what happens to you. You must remain focus on the final result. Most successful people in the world today did not just achieve success in one day, in actual fact, successful people usually go through a long journey before they arrive, and there are various levels of activities that they go through. Most times is what they conceive in their minds, and that is where it all begins, they thought of something, they thought over it over some period of time, they began seeing the possibility of bringing it to life, they start the process, from one process to another, in science, it is idea, knowledge, hypothesis, methodology, experiment, theory and conclusion.

These activities are geared towards knowing something and bringing it to existence and if it does work out, then it becomes a generally accepted phenomenon. Therefore, you need to understand that successful people usually go through some stages and activities that actually shape their destiny, take for instance people who are into sports. They usually enroll in one academy or the other, and the basics of the sports is being thought, the ones that get the vision will quickly start the processing in their brains and it gradually settles down into them. The skill and the nifty gritty of the sports are exposed to them, the coaches or trainers begin to discover the talents and that is it, and the individual involved captures and develops it in the brain.

The process begins with knowing and having the opportunity to be exposed to the trainings that will make you have the mind that you just have to keep on doing what you are doing, and that may not come easy because in every aspect of the games there is always rigorous or regular trainings, the trainings carried out is to enable you to compete in difficult situations, the rudiment of the sports activities is put through to you and you have to undergo it in the hands of those people who are out to make you know it.

Sometimes these activities needs sacrifice and discipline, you will need to remain positive and keep on going, following the basics and know it.

In every of the activities, there are always rules and regulations, you will need to stay and keep to it or else you will lose touch of the whole idea. Being resilient means that; you must know and develop the attitude that will help you to stay in touch with the purpose of the course.

It demands a lot of sacrifice when it comes to being resilient, many people give up easily when they fail at the quest of something, depending on the area, if you fail an examination for instance or you failed an interview for instance, you shouldn't feel that it's the end of the world. No! you need to pick up yourself and continue, try again, keep trying and work hard to pass it the next time, that you fail in your first attempt doesn't mean you will not pass the next one.

Failure is only a Postponed success

If you are doing business and you have failed to establish your brand, and your company is winding up, don't lose hope, because you only discovered one way of attaining success, yes! That is the way I term it, when you fail in business, know that others also failed in their attempts, if you do a research you will discover that many people who started business actually got their fingers burnt, they fail in their first attempt at getting the business running. So don't give up, you need to bounce back and get it going. That you fail in one particular business doesn't mean you will not succeed in another business.

If you are schooling and you don't get to pass your examination, don't worry, if you fail, hey! Failure is only a postpone success, take a look at the records of the guy who scored the highest mark, take a look at his or her result and say to it, if this is what someone did, I can score a better mark, start working towards it and achieve it, beat it, be the boy or girl to beat, stand out, you are the best at what you do, if you don't be the best nobody will help you to be the best except the one who is helping you to get there as your mentor.

The ability to receive shock or disappointments

Before you can be a resilient person, it begins with your mindset, when your mind is prepared already, you will be able to receive whatever comes to you. To be that tough minded individual, it takes a lot of training and the orientation you get will determine how far you will be able to go. Your orientation matters because except you get the right orientation, you will not make it to advance in mental toughness.

Being resilient can be tested when you receive a shock from what goes on around you, if you have been stressed up already and someone is trying to frustrate you the more, and you do not care and still believe you can overcome any obstacle place before you; then you can trust that you are mentally strong. People go through difficult times, when such a person gets into difficult situation that tends to break him or her, the person doesn't give up and maintain a high level of optimism and finds solutions to the problem that person has a strong mentality.

You are hit by something that tends to weaken you, something that can make you cry, something that can make you feel the whole world is crashing, but you are able to stand your ground and face the problem and completely obliterate or take control of the situation, that means you are mentally strong.

If you get into a situation that can devastate you and you are able to force your way back on track while you move on with your daily activity without feeling bad about the situation, you are in the right state of being resilient. Resilient is something that keeps you coming back after a fall or misfortune. When some people meet misfortune in their lives they may not continue with their regular activities, they tend to be easily disappointed when such things happen. That means that person is not resilient, but if there is anything that happens to a person and the person keeps on moving, the person is unfazed by what happens to him or her, that person is resilient.

I have watched a football match sometime in 1989 held in one of the Asian countries it was a very difficult match during the semi final of the FIFA underage competition, the under 21 world cup, at half time one of the team was four nil down. At the resumption of the second half, the psychologist's strategy was employed on the loosing team; they were being encouraged that they have the potential of coming back into the game. And when they got to the second half, they played and just about fifteen minutes to the end of the match the goals started coming in, by the ninetieth minute three goals had been replied back and at ninety two minutes, there was an equalizer. From four goals down in the first half and just about fifteen minutes to the end of the match a miracle had taken place, the match ended up in penalties and the team who believed so much in themselves who stayed strong and resilient got the victory at the end of the extra time. Why did this happen? Is none other than resilience, if the loosing team gave up the fight before the end of the second half as most team do, they wouldn't have achieve such feet. Even if when one of the athletes got injured, the team still went ahead and won the match, it was a pyrrhic victory, and that match is still being talked about hitherto.

Resilience is one characteristic that an individual should make serious efforts at inculcating because your ability to be resilient will help in giving you success whenever the moment comes.

Again another example is one popular American wrestler called Shawn Michaels, he was later nick named the Heart Break Kid, why? Because he was a very good example of a resilient athlete, Shawn will enter the ring with a lot of confidence against his opponents, he wasn't a big guy, he was average but with a big heart, Shawn was known for his ability to go a very long distance with his opponents, even if Shawn's opponent were usually bigger in size, Shawn would receive a beating for several minutes or hours but yet his opponent will not be able to pin him, Shawn's resilience usually weakens his opponents, he was very good at frustrating his opponents and then at the end the opponents will tire out and Shawn will take advantage and inflict a defeat on his opponent. This was how Shawn became a specialist in being resilient, and he got the status as the "heart break kid" because he was able to cause several upset on his unsuspected opponents who had thought he would be easy to beat. He was just an average size guy, but his resilience became a trademark, he defeated many bigger wrestlers.

Your resilience will always make you to defeat your situation and circumstances, believe it. Learn to be resilient; I'll give you the story of a little dog and a bigger dog. Once upon a time, there was this small dog which usually leaves his little house and goes to meet a bigger dog in the neighboring house and start barking at it. The bigger dog will come out and beat it up and the smaller dog will run away back to its little house, the next day the little dog will go back and start a fight, the big dog comes out to beat it up and the small dog will go back home, the next day the small dog comes out to start a fight, it went on like that daily until the bigger dog became tired of the small dog, the big dog left his house for the small dog and never came back.

That is the power of resilience, remember the definition of resilience, being able to withstand obstacle without being permanently devastated. The little dog actually wanted to take over the house of the big dog, and it used its own mental toughness, its own mental toughness against that of the big dog and the small dog won the battle irrespective of the number of times it got beaten and overpowered during the daily fights. The small dog had a purpose, it remained focused on achieving its aim and objectives, and it did not stop harassing the big dog until it got what it wanted.

You may be passing through difficult moments, things may not be working well for you, but stay focus and continue to work hard to change that situation, take the bull by the horn, just like the small dog, it took the big dog on a very long journey, using its own resilience, the small dog was able to break the big dog's size into small pieces, just because of its resilience.

So, whatever you do in life, be resilient, if you are a student and you are trying hard to pass your exams and you failed in more than one attempt, what you have to do is to start reading hard and prepare better, burn the mid night candle, be consistent and persistent with your study, while others are playing and wasting their precious times on things that will not add value to their studies. You can chose to go to the library to study more, read harder and improve on yourself; these are activities that show resilience in education.

If you are a businessman or woman, you have problems taking your business to the next level, don't get discourage, all you need is to re-strategize, take your time to look inward, discover where your business is not doing well and improve on it, take the necessary action to strengthen that area of your business that is weak, if it is something that has to do with promotion, work out your budget, if it is getting the right professionals into positions that will exploit their talents for the benefit or growth of the business, get the right professionals to handle the job, if it is the area that needs the right candidate or employees to fill vacant positions, get them to work and decide what to do with them to make your business grow faster.

Work out your budget to run your business, many corporate organizations get into problems associated with tax and overhead cost, floating a business sometimes can be very cumbersome, the early stages of business organization is often marred with great challenges, some business start small and they move gradually, others start big and soon come crashing and end up winding up. Most companies start small and follow the proven strategies to grow bigger.

Most individuals that lead industrial revolution or advancement are actually people with better mental toughness, when they present their proposals to banks, they are able to get the necessary start up capitals because the banks may see through their mental strength their ability to deliver when given the loans. Most times these people with mental toughness have already established business which is already doing well, they get credit for that and the bank trust their resilience at succeeding and they often get loans to expand their businesses.

The secret of being resilient

One of the top secret when a person is resilient is the fact that resilience will always lead to success, because the more you keep working at something, the more you keep doing that thing, you keep practicing it, you keep on performing that thing, you get the highest chance of attaining perfection at what you are doing.

Study other people who are Resilient

You need to start studying other people who are resilient, you'll be able to know how this people are making things happen with their ability to become resilient at what they are doing, we have a lot of people who have become legend because of their being resilient, no matter what challenge before you, you have the ability to succeed and become successful, when you study others, you will be able to determine their strength and how their story began and how they were able to achieve or what they have achieved so far as they have become very resilient.

Be Patient

Don't be in a rush to get something that you are looking for, am not saying you should quit but rather, work out things strategically with proven methods as employed in this book, you've heard from the old saying that the patient dog will eat the fattest bone, why? because while other dogs were fighting for the bone, they fought each other and forgot the bone, and while they were busy fighting the patient dog just walked in and took the bone away, if the later joined in the fight, it will never get the bone, some other dog will come and take it away, but while the other dogs were fighting, the patient dog just planned and strategized, watching the other dogs fighting and forgetting the bones and it just went and took the big bone and left.

Think about it, whatever you are looking for in life, you should plan and take a different method that others aren't taking. There is always one way to achieving success and when you follow it you will get there.

Patience therefore is one characteristics of a person who is mentally tough, you will notice that they always plan ahead in any of their activities that they involved themselves in. Being patient will enable you to see through things very clearly and what decision is to be taken when faced with stiff challenges.

Be focus in realizing your dream

A lot of people actually lose focus and easily get distracted away from getting to the point of success; this is where I am going to make you understand that being focus is a way of improving on your mental toughness. Let me share from the popular experience of one athlete in the track and field. He is a house hold name, an Olympic champion by merit, he has been tested and trusted and he has been put through screening and he doesn't have any issues with drug cheating, he never used drug enhancing performance to excel in his field. His name is Husain Bolt, this man broke his own record at the Olympics and today he stands tall among his pairs, when he was interviewed he responded and said "whenever he starts a race his focus is on the gold medal".

He categorically stated that "whenever the sound of the whistle is blown and the race starts, he doesn't care about who or what his competitors are, all that is in his mind at that moment is the gold medal", somehow, that has worked for him over the years, he is known for his multiple gold medal winning streaks during his debut in the Olympic games.

That is the mind of a champion; a champion doesn't gets distracted by the caliber of his fellow competitors or contemporaries in the business.

Husain has over the years maintain a healthy level of concentration and that has really worked for him. If you are into anything that has to do with great productivity, always try your possible best to be focused.

What does it take to be focused?

To remain focused is to remain in total concentration towards the goal that you set out to achieve without allowing yourself to be distracted with what is happening in your environment.

It doesn't matter what anybody says about what you are planning to do or what you are doing to achieve success, being resilient is what matters because if you succeed you are going to be the one that will be affected and celebrated if you decide to fail you are still going to get mocked at. So why don't you take the right decision by staying focus on your goals so you can achieve it. You need to passionately pursue your goals by staying focus.

Focus in the field of science always refers to a particular spot, in physics for instance, when we talk about focus, we talking about the point where there is a convergence or concentration. But however, in real life situation we are almost reasoning along the same line with the scientist, focusing on a particular goal that must be or can be achieved is what makes us to have the mental capacity and toughness to achieve it. Especially, when we are living in a contemporary society where there is competition for space, business or to dominate the market. When there is a prize at stake, we always have the first position, second position and the third position and others prizes to be won. Everyone will have to compete for the top spot.

Take for instance the FIFA world cup, that comes up once in every four years, the thirty four teams that usually compete always want to win the first prize, every country wants to lift the FIFA world cup, that is the biggest achievement in the world of football, but the first spot is only for one country. Hence, there is always stiff competition; a team that wants to win must stay focus.

I have witnessed great teams who have the potentials of winning the world cup, but something will come up within the team, either one player is having problems with the coach or a team having problem with the National handlers, they tend to seek for their demands, which may be disagreements on bonuses to be paid to the players or allowances, this can cause a serious disunity in the team. The team eventually lost focus and will never play to its potential, thereby getting eliminated in the early stages of the competition.

Being focus is inevitable because it will enable you to remain in the course of the team's quest to win the competition. So also it is in real life situation, if you lost focus on what you intend to achieve with what you are doing, you will miss the mark of success and get on the wrong side of life, and such is the case associated with people who lose focus on what they are doing.

You will never see someone who has mental toughness losing focus, because if they do, they will never achieve that which makes them to be champions. Again, I'll show you example of a young man in the world of football whom

I perceived and I've studied him for the last decade and I come to conclusion, that to me, he is still the number one player, that is the person when it comes to being focus. He is no other than Lionel Messi of Argentina, I've noticed that in every game, this young man has always remain focused, I've watched him played for FIFA underage competition and with his present club, FC Barcelona, this young man has always been focused, he never allows a minute to pass without staying focus, other teams who have faced him always have the inability to remain focus and they often get punished by this young man, the way he plays, he attaches seriousness to it and that ability to remain focused all the time during games has made him to become an enigma in his chosen career.

Lionel doesn't change his style of play, he is still the same old Messi that every team in the La Liga knows, how come they have not been able to study his style of play and cut his ability to get past them, it's simply because of one thing called focus and resilience.

When you are resilient other team don't need to be very excellent at stopping you, you are the one that will determine if you can be stopped or not, you remember the story of the small dog, it was constantly doing what it believes will defeat the big dog and it did achieve its aim. To be focus therefore will be able to determine your mental toughness. People who are always focused at achieving something always end up achieving what they are looking for. Like the old saying "shoot for the sun and you may end up being among the stars". This is a very true statement, you will not only end up being among the stars, you will be the shining light or sun if you really stay focus and resilient.

Focus is all about concentration, ask yourself the following question:

How often have I stayed focused in the course of my goals?

Have you ever written down your goals and focused on it?

Have you ever thought about achieving something positive?

Have you thought about greatness?

What do you know about the people who are great in this world?

What do you think they have done to achieve greatness?

Is there a way possible to achieve greatness, just like other people in the world?

If you must look inwards you will discover that there may be a vacuum in your life, and that vacuum needs to be filled up. It takes you and a reliable mentor to guide you to reach that goal.

When you stay focus, it means that you have driven away from you all distraction, there is nothing anybody will say to you that will affect you, you will become like a solid rock that cannot be moved from a particular spot to another, it doesn't matter the number of times you might have failed in your previous attempts, the main theme is for you to act right in any circumstances and that will propel you to victory. In today's world, many people fade away simply because there was no one to give them a pep talk, no one to give them the needed inspiration to excel in their various life endeavors, no one to help them remain focused.

Your level of success will be determined by the level of concentration quotient that you have, whenever the time comes for you to remain focused, always try as much as possible to stay in control of your senses. Whenever there is a stiff competition, the people who stay focus and follow the directives of the coaches or trainer are always the ones who end up doing well.

As you read, I'll love you to take notes of the salient points which have to do with being focus, make sure you are able to develop your level of concentration which plays a big role in your quest at achieving a stronger mental development.

Now there is something that you must take note of, and that is, what do you do when there is distraction?

I know by now you might have been thinking when I said you must be focused, does it mean you'll never get distracted, not at all, distraction will always come to you, It's something we all cannot avoid, whether you stay away from distraction, remember you are not a lonely island, everyday you will have to interact with people around you, and that will always lead to distractions.

If you are schooling or in a corporate environment, you meet different people every day and whatever transpires between you and them comes to the table when there is conflict. In every human interaction, the likelihood of getting yourself in a disagreement is higher and that's why we need to get ourselves abreast with the various acts of communication between various individuals that cuts across the society and this is what we are making you to understand. Despite the various interactions that we have, the need to stay and keep in touch with our major goal is very important.

For you to remain focused in life you'll need to have certain qualities which are:

- Never allow yourself to be intimidated by your opponents.

- never give in to distractions

- don't allow other people's success get into your head

- your own success is much more important than others

- no one is better than you, you are the best at what you do

- believe the fact that there is competition

- believe that you alone is the best and you must beat your own records

- don't allow your past experiences to get into your head

- see yourself as the champion who has won the competition or title already

- your fellow competitors are not better than you

- think about becoming the last man standing

When you begin to think in this manner, there is every possibility that you will definitely win or come close to winning. This mentality level of thinking will always make you to stay ahead among your pears, because your thinking will propel you to break your own records, once you are able to do this, then your level of focus has improved and better prepared for the next level.

Learn from the Mistakes of Others

Being resilient is excellent when you do not repeat the same mistakes others did. When you study people who have become successful, you need to also know or study their critical situation, such as what made them become more successful than others and you also need to study why they failed at a certain point in their life, and when they did fail, you ask questions to know if they actually did rise again to former glories, if they did not rise from their failure, find out why and what kept them from getting back to their previous winning ways.

You will be shocked to find out that most successful people who failed had one problem or the other that led to their downfall, so if you want to stay ahead and become a better champion, you need to maintain a certain level of knowledge about successful people who made it big and suddenly fall back to oblivion.

Don't give room for Complacency

Being complacent is a way of thinking that you have arrived at the best spot in your life, it is a time that makes you feel comfortable with what you have achieve and therefore you decide to rest. This can be very dangerous, because just when you think you have accomplished what you are looking for or competing for, some other persons or team is actually following you and are working had to overtake you. Therefore if you must remain mentally tough you don't need to give room for complacency, being resilient is when you are not complacent, you decide not to rest until you achieve. Sometimes people tend to relax on the numeral laurels, they are so contented with what they have, for instance, if an athlete wins a tournament or competition, it happened because he or the team prepared very well and they won. They won because their mentality was high, they believed they could win and they played to their highest potential. But the same team comes back in two years time to compete in the same competition and they have a minnow or underrated team, if they feel that they can easily walk over the underrated team, and then they could as well be plotting their own elimination.

Teams always prepare and it is possible with the right mental toughness any team in a competition stands a chance to lift the trophy, so if you want to have mental toughness you must not give room for complacency.

In the corporate world, companies may start business and begin to grow gradually, as the year roles by the company can record huge success and it can be doing well in the market, but when the income generated is not well managed to help in expanding the horizon of the company, it may find itself struggling with any competitor who is better prepared to take over the market.

Constant training and research is being deployed by big and smaller organization to ensure they continuously improve their business to maximize profit, no matter the success of a company, there should be no avenue or giving of room for complacency to negatively affect the business organization.

In education, when a student rest and stop studding, the student may likely begin to forget what he or she has learnt over the period of his or her education, when the examination is close by, the confidence will not be there if such student cannot read, therefore there should be no room for complacency while you are undergoing your educational pursuit. You need to be ahead of the class then continue your study, you want to be the best student then spend more of your time reading and doing research on your study. You want to score the highest grade? you'll need to go the extra mile to get the needed results.

I have also noticed in the present world of technological advancement, companies involved in the manufacturing industry have been carrying out various grades of technological equipment production, some have been doing well while some of them have fizzle out among the top manufacturers. Companies which have fared better always become successful because they are able to vision the winning mentality and the right mental toughness to supersede their competitors.

That is why you can see the volumes of quality products coming from these companies. Hence, with resilience even when business is doing well, they kept on believing that it's going to work and it did work for them, that is the same kind of mentality you should have as an individual or owner of a business. Always maintain that you are going to break records, that you are going to make it big and eventually become successful.

Take note of the following key points:

- Always believe you are just starting

- Don't think you have won anything even if you have won actually

- Don't underestimate your opponent

- don't change your belief

- belief that you are going to win

- stay faithful to the course

- see yourself winning already before the game begins

- try as much as you can to break your own records

- stay united to the game plan

- work in unity with the other members of the team

- remove the thoughts of weakness from your mind

- play to your biggest potentials

- use what you have to achieve your dreams

- cooperate with other members of the team

- stay calm and focus on what you want to achieve

- do not show signs of tiring out

- if you get tired, have a little rest to recuperate

- always plan your actions

- strategize a winning formula that will make you successful

- respect other competitors but make sure you have an edge over them

- go the extra mile to do what others aren't doing

Non-negotiable Fight Back

After you have successfully develop a level of discernment, you are gradually building your mental toughness, and it is becoming obvious that you have been setting up yourself and ready to improve. One things comes your way and that is sudden shock, how tough are you to receive sock, remember to be resilient, you must be able to receive shock and you should be able to respond positively, any situation or circumstances that inflicts shock on you, the way you respond to it will determine how mentally tough you are, for instance, when you get a bad news about your business, maybe your business is about to crash or suffers a big loss, how do you respond to such. When such thing happens to you which may be a misfortune, all you need to do is to accept the fact that something unfortunate has happened.

If you accept that fact, then the next thing you should be thinking about is how to get out of those ugly circumstances, that is the right step in the right direction. I have seen some people when they experience a misfortune, the way they react is somewhat terrible, all you see them do is start crying over spilt milk. Crying never solves a problem, rather it further aggravates the tension surrounding the problem, crying encourages a state of being hopeless, like there is no solution to the problem.

To be resilient in that circumstances, you need to start fighting back, whatever the problem is, begin by proffering the options you have to bring about the solution to such problem. Being resilient is what keep you going and when you begin to reason that nothing can actually break you, not even your spirit can be broken when you are resilient. I don't know if you understand when your resilient is so stubborn that your opponent feels threatened by your presence, this I have seen happens to many people.

So, when you remain resolute, it's time for you to fight back, you do this by facing the problem, start looking for solution, see it as one of the situation when a man has to stand up and face reality, you can do it and nothing can stop you from achieving your goal.

The Israelite while they were moving out of Egypt, the great exodus, it didn't happen without them facing challenges, they got to a point of no return, it was the Israelite facing the red sea and at the same time being pursued by Pharaoh's army. That was the point they were faced with difficult situation and they were afraid, some of the people started blaming Moses for bringing them into their doom, they began to remember the life in Egypt, at that moment, they would prefer to remain in Egypt rather than getting their freedom from slavery.

What you should understand here is that, at certain point, you get discouraged you begin to get the temptation of giving up on your dreams, you forget how far you have come and you want to give up everything. Remember, the same thing happened to the Israelite. But how did Moses receive the shock and fact that they stood in front of the red sea without any means to cross, while the Egyptian armies were fast approaching. What did Moses do? He started by calming the people down and reminded them of the God that they served. Now Moses started by calming down, secondly he began to calm the noise around him, for in the midst of confusion or chaos, there is no solution there, the noise will make you to lose concentration, you will easily get distracted and you will never see the possibility of turning your situation into a successful one. Thereafter Moses switched and also helped the people to remember what they believe in. The Israelite believed they have a God, but at that very moment many of them did not believe in their God, they believed they would perished at the hands of the Egyptian armies and that there was no way they could cross the red sea. Moses set a very good example of resilience, he knew that there was always a way, because his mental toughness never failed him, his mental toughness was linked to his believe in the God of Israel and that was a powerful means of breaking loose and escaping from the hands of the Israelites, the resilience of Moses brought down the power of God to divide the red sea and the Israelite went across the sea to the other end.

If Moses did not fall back on what he believed, there was no way he would have gotten any result.

Moses was outstanding among the Israelite because he was operating in a different level of mentality which other Israelite did not have, Moses was prepared for the exodus journey, he had so many encounters in his life, from the time he was a baby. So, everything that you need to become mentally resilient has to do with your development.

The Israelite once again showed their mental weakness when they cried out to Moses that the Egyptian army were successfully coming after them when the Israelite found out that they had crossed to the other side of the red sea.

Still they did not believe that they can never be captured by the Egyptians. Sometime these situation will happen to you in life, these are moments that touches your level of mental toughness, unlike Moses, the Israelites kept on complaining, always lacking the believe, always showing their mental weakness, always displaying naivety, despite all the miracles done through Moses, they still were overwhelmed by fear of being captured.

It took the mental toughness of Moses and his believe in the God that he served to bring back the divided Nile to close in on the Egyptian and that was their doom.

Listen, it is not what is happening to you that matters, the real deal is you, you are the one being affected by what is going on around you, the way you respond to that situation is what will make people evaluate your mental toughness, that is the simple truth, you cannot say you are resilient and you don't believe in the possibility of getting something done, you can't claim to be mentally tough or being resilient and you complain about everything that comes your way that appears to be causing you misfortune, the time to start thinking that you can actually overcome any problem is now.

Hence, you have to fight back, you have to fight the misfortune without relenting, like the Egyptians who chased Moses, Moses fought back by what he knew and believe in, the Pharaoh depended on his army, but Moses depended on his God, he depended on Him with his believe and Mental toughness, Moses was resilient to the hot chase of the Egyptians and he defeated them.

To be resilient therefore, you need to learn the simple basic things that will go a long way to aid your mental toughness:

- Learn to fight back

- Don't stay down

- Develop a diehard spirit

- Believe in what you've got

- Unleash what you have got

- Do not be deterred by your followers or people around you who don't believe in what you believe

- Call out that powers within you

How Determination to Succeed causes you to become resilient

A man who doesn't have any ambition or plan on how he can succeed in life has a mental weakness. He needs to realize his potential and aim higher and he can only do this when he has a better improved mental toughness.

How determination does cause you to become resilient? There is one factor that is common to successful people who have mental toughness and that thing is "determination".

Determination is like an infection in the mind of a man or woman who wants to become mentally tough, when you are determined to the extent that you always see yourself already living the life that you want to live, when you see yourself receiving the trophy or gold medal of success, when you want to become a doctor, lawyer, entrepreneur, successful business man or woman, or a champion in sports, you do things that will gradually move you close and eventually becoming what you want to be, then you are determined, you deserve it.

It beats my imagination when I see people who live the life of pauper, I see a lot of people who are poor and what baffles me the most is the fact that they are undecided and they just don't care to know why they are living a very pitiable life. People who just accept their fate and remain where they are for many years without any signs of improvement are just not determined to change their situation.

If you truly desire to make a change, change will always come your way, and that can only happen if you are determined to achieve the goal, there are no two ways about determination. Believe me if there is another way other than determination, a lot of people will follow that path. Sometimes I'm amused when people talk about luck, yes! It's true you may have been lucky, but you cannot be lucky all the time, that's why you will hear from a popular saying which goes as thus "don't always count on your luck".

Those who are determined to get something have something within which drives them to success; it has to do with what they believe in and how they are really interested to get it. Determination will make you to get something that you want by all cost; determination is a driving force that will propel you to advance towards your goal. If you listen to the interviews of some famous people around the world, barely will you see anyone who got anything by chance, am not saying there are no people who fall into that category, no! What I mean is that some great people actually achieve what they dreamed of by being determined to get that thing which they cherish most.

So if you are living in today's world and you are not determined to succeed, then you need to start thinking differently, you need to increase or start nursing your determination to succeed.

Determination is one of the characteristics of being resilient and that is the bedrock of advancement towards achieving your goal.

To be able to be a determined person, you have to do the following things;

- Be resolute to achieve your goal

- Write out what you are determined to get

- Start your day by committing to doing things that will help you achieve your goals

- Think about your level of determination and evaluate yourself

- Each day write out what you have been able to achieve while you were determined

- Create time for silent meditation

- Visualize yourself to have already achieve your dream goals

- Work towards achieving your goal

- Be consistent

- Be active

Get the required Motivation

To be resilient you will need motivation, to successfully achieve that mental toughness by becoming resilient, you need to keep up the level, once you decline in your level of motivation; it will be very difficult to achieve your target goals. Every individual in the world today need to have the right source of motivation which should always be the positive one. That positive motivation will make you develop the drive towards becoming resilient and achieve mental toughness.

Motivation can be achieved by some activities such as desire, listening to motivational speakers, having a mentor etc. if you increase your desire of achieving something great, you will need a form of motivation, motivation can bring out the very best in you, when you have someone who guides you through, we have quite a lot of motivational speakers like Warren Buffet, Robert Kiyosaki, Donald Trump, Bill Gates etc.

These people are successful people who usually give out motivational speech and trainings that will help you get the highest level of resilience and mental toughness to succeed in any area of your chosen career.

They are not difficult to access, they have lots of their speech and trainings on YouTube and you can find them on social media, they usually give out their speeches on these platforms and you can listen to them or purchase their books and read to get motivated.

Motivation is the spice you need in your life when everything seems not to be working, when you are motivated, you can go to any length to achieving success, but success will not come if you are not motivated to achieve success in your life, so always get motivated in anything that you are doing, if you cannot read, you can simply download motivational videos from video websites and you will get a lot of popular people who are into motivational speech delivering quality services on various video sites and networks.

Motivation gives you the extra push to believe in your ability to succeed, being resilient is what makes you tough and people who are very tough will survive in all weather. The problem of many people is that they lack the needed motivation to move ahead of their pairs, learning is something that we acquire from the colleges and schools, but motivation is something that has to do with helping you to succeed and get the necessary result, most people require some form of push, some get it easily some just don't get it easily, you need to urge them on, you need to inspire them and that is exactly what happens around the world, in today's world we have champions and we also have people who are not champions but mere performers, for instance, if you look at many football leagues from different countries, you will notice the difference in some teams more than others, there are teams who have high potential of winning games and they always show in their games that they will win and they play better than others.

When teams get motivated they can perform at their best. Some may get motivated with monetary promises or rewards and it works out for them and that usually gives them the extra push to attain success.

I'll advice that you don't depend on monetary rewards for you to get motivated. Because motivation should be gotten from a natural source, that is by the spoken words, that long old method is what has proven to be very effective, listen and hear the words of motivation and that will be the necessary tonic that you need.

When you are listening to motivational speakers, make sure you write down the points that you really need to understand.

What you should do:

- Create time to listen to motivational speakers

- Get a pen and a notepad to jot down important information

- Attend seminars and workshops

- Don't focus on the money, focus on the motivation and the money will come

- Get yourself acquainted with a motivational speaker

Having a very Strong Ambition

Ambition is the act of aspiring to acquire something that you cherish or hold in high esteemed, it is the desire of an individual to achieve that gratifying status or thing that will become fulfilling. Many people around the world live and die without fulfilling their dreams. It may not be their fault but simply because there was no strong ambition.

If you believe that you can achieve anything in life, then you can work your ambition to the level where you will be able to get anything that you want.

Ambition is one of the driving force to propels resilience, when your ambition is constantly emphatic in your mind and you desire it like it is something you must get at all cost, with the right attitude, be rest assured you will get there in no distant time. It's only a matter of time before you know it your desires will be fulfilled, hence, in whatever you do always have some level of ambition, let it be a healthy one, there are ambition that can be too extreme. For example, if you desire a big position in a company, all you need to do is to work towards achieving it, simply do what others aren't doing, earned the position on merit not by politicking or maneuvering and eliminating your competitor in the organization. Your uprightness and extra ordinary approach to your job will earn you the promotions that will advance you to get to that level. That is something that is very important, you should take that seriously.

If you lack the ambition to get something that is desirable, you will never get it easily. Lack of ambition will only leave you day dreaming about something without getting it. I've notice that the ambition factor is what is not available in the lives of most people.

Michael Jordan was once told during his early years as an amateur basketball player that he lacks what it takes to play basket ball, this statement baffled Michael Jordan, he was told he cannot play, he took the information and processed it in his brain.

While he was sitting feeling rejected, he thought in his mind, what is it that is so special about these guys that have been chosen to play and him left out and not selected to play.

Michael Jordan went home, he became more ambitious and vowed to proof the team handlers wrong, his ambition spur him to do extra training, and he developed his skills, he moved on despite his previous disappointments, he worked hard and got back to reckoning, today in the United states of America and all over the world, you cannot mention Basketball without talking about the name Michael Jordan, Jordan became a household name, he proved his critiques wrong, he rose from a no body to become somebody, his coaches who told him few years back that he is not fit to play basketball watch and saw him become very famous and being among the very best ever seen in the sports and also top earner.

Michael Jordan showed resilience when he refused to accept his critique's opinion, and that goes forth to show that other people's opinion doesn't count when it comes to your capabilities, your mental strength doesn't depend on their own opinion, you are different and you can write your own history. Michael Jordan wrote his own history and he had no option than to leave an indelible mark in the basketball history. Whatever you are today can be transformed into something great, you are just a raw gold, until you discover yourself, you will definitely shine and find a place among the stars.

Become resilient by becoming ambitious about what you want to achieve or become. I will give you another example in the person of one skilful football player called Ronaldinho, one of brazil's famous playmaker and master tricksters in the world of football.

Ronaldinho in his early days in football pleaded with his coach while he was on trial in Portugal to play him. The coach refused and blatantly told Ronaldinho that he doesn't have the height to play football. Sad, disappointed and feeling dejected, Ronaldinho went on to develop his skills, he later became the world's best player on two occasions and he was noted for his trademark skills.

Since Ronaldinho is no longer playing international football, his skillful dexterity has been greatly missed as it seems no one was able to re-enact his mesmerizing skills.

Ronaldinho was ambitious to use what he has to get what he wanted, he was absolutely an entertaining player to watch and he exploited his potential by being resilient and committed to his ambition. And that is why he is a respected player in the world of football. What do you think happened to the coach who refused to sign Ronaldinho, sighting the fact that he didn't have the heights to play football, the said coach was voted the worst coach in the world, why? Because he lacked the foresight to see the talent and potentials of Ronaldinho while he was yet to be established player.

This is the lesson you need to know from the above, you see, when you are raw, you are just like a gold which has not been refined, what do I mean? I'm saying that when you have not gotten any training, when you have not started having ambition about what you really want, you are just like a raw gold which has not been refined. Until you begin to build your ambition, then you will notice that your goals will continue to develop and become clearer to you. Ambition therefore is something that propels an individual to constantly want something and the person will work towards it, while he or she does that, the tendency that the recurrent attributes of getting that thing becomes an attitude that will always spur you on, the resilient factor begins to become a characteristic akin to your mindset and that is one thing that can drive you to excel in your career.

Ambition therefore is what will help in improving your resilience and your mental toughness will become much more prominent with your Ambitious tendencies.

Having the Vision

When you have a vision of what you are doing which is basically futuristic, you will go far in having the mental toughness, why? Because you will not be thinking short term but all you know now is long term, for example, I'll give you instances of people around the world who have been successful with what they are doing; it all began with a vision. These great individuals did not just start doing something just because they wanted to do something that will keep them busy, rather, they saw the power and great potential in what they are inventing and when it comes to actualization it can serve a greater purpose.

A visionary has the ability to see into the future success of what he or she is doing. The two brothers who invented aero plane sat down together to think of what they can do to achieve what they had seen in a vision about flying humans from one place to another through the air and they made it manifest and today they are regarded as great individuals, when you lack vision, it means you cannot fulfill life's given opportunities. The visionary will see through the future of anything that he or she is doing, when you are able to vision yourself and see beyond the ordinary then you can be rest assured that success will gradually develop in your mind, because you will dream to achieve everything that you vision about.

Bill Gates thought of something that can create an interface between humans, something that can cause a file transmission that can cut across one country to another and from one continent to another via the internet, he discovered a software and made it possible to be accessed by anyone from anywhere in the world via the internet file transfer protocol and it worked.

The whole process started by conceiving the idea and vision, today, all the computers in the world or every individual or business organization is using Microsoft office software to carry out various data processing that is beneficial to individuals and corporate organization or various institutions. There is no doubt that Bill Gates and the likes of other people had a vision to contribute their knowledge to the growing population of the world by simply discovering a file transmitting and processing channel that will be accessible from anywhere in the world.

Today Bill can be regarded as one of the most strongest persons with the right mental toughness that we have in the world today considering his background, when his project and idea was rejected by other established firms, while he sought to sell his idea to them, he wasn't bothered about their rejection of his proposal, he simply went on to develop his capabilities and discoveries and he earned his success by believing in the vision that he had actually shared with others who never cared to buy into his idea.

Before your vision can work for you, you ought to believe in the vision, know that you are the one to see into the future of your proposed idea. It starts from you, it doesn't depend whether others buy into it or not, rather you'll be the one to shoulder much responsibility of your believe and the vision that comes with other activities will definitely spur you to conquer what there has to be defeated on your way to success. Ask yourself the following question:

- Do I have a vision?

- What is my vision?

- Can I sustain my vision?

- What will I do to sustain my vision?

- Do you see the vision of yourself in the next one year, two years, three, years, five years and above?

- Will I be able to get my vision across to others

- Will others understand what I dream about

- Can I impact into other people's life with my vision

- When am I going to realize my vision

- When and where will I achieve my vision

- Can you evaluate yourself on what you have been able to achieve with your current vision.

Don't leave a life without a vision, have a daily vision, have monthly vision, have a quarterly vision, have a yearly vision and long term vision accordingly.

Chapter 4

Self-Discipline & Willpower on Demand

Discipline is the training, teaching or learning that tends to perfects the mental faculties or moral character, it is a control gained by enforcing obedience or order, it is also a orderly or prescribed conduct or pattern of behavior, self control and also a system of rules governing conduct or activity.

From the above definition, every individual who possesses any of the above features is capable of having self discipline, self discipline is very important in the mental toughness in today's world. The issue now is to ask yourself the big question, do I have self discipline?

The answer is not contained in only saying "yes". Having self discipline cuts across all the areas of your life, the way you behave, what you say, what you do every day which also includes what you eat, your lifestyle and the kind of friends you keep, the kind of places you go to all determine how disciplined you are.

Many people in the world today have been destroyed by lack of discipline, when you are not disciplined, there are so many things that can happen to you which can negatively impact your life.

When you are not disciplined you will miss opportunities, remember that taking opportunities can only happen if you identify one and secondly not only identifying an opportunity but also having the mental discernment and key into such opportunity. Those who take opportunity are those who actually see through it. Opportunities always present itself to more than two or more people but only those with a better mental attitude will key into it.

When Bill Gates started his project, he invited some of his friends to participate, there were many of them, but in the end, only ten people actually keyed into the opportunity and today they are proud to be part of that project. What happened to the rest, of course they were not interested, such a mental weakness to see a great opportunity that lies in the future or something that is about to transform your life, your inability to see it also comes from your low mental state or weakness, you were just not disciplined enough to see it.

Self discipline will make you understand situation and get connected to opportunities when you see one.

Self discipline will make you to avoid what causes scandal in the life of men or women. A man who is disciplined will hardly get connected with scandal, for instance, we have had some famous athletes who involved themselves in cheating, such as is seen in the world of indoor and outdoor sports around the world, drug related offences which has destroyed the career of many athletes often happen from time to time. During Olympic competition and other competitions we have seen players and athletes who always fail drug test. Sad enough many athletes do not learn from the mistakes of the fallen heroes who fall along the line of failing drug test, they sometimes fall along the line to the same offences.

To be disciplined you need to understand certain things, one of the way you see life shouldn't be winning at all cost, you should see life as a process, not what you see that must be gotten immediately within your grasp, you can desire something, but at the same time you need to wait patiently to get it, sometimes you need to do away with certain things than others. To be disciplined, you must be vigilant to be able to identify traps that can cause your down fall. You have to "live like a lion to scare away your enemies and be cunning like hyena to identify traps". This is the simple summary of being discipline.

If you are an employee, there is something that is called responsibility in a company; it's the usual practice in many business organizations that there should be rules and regulations. No employer is going to employ someone who will not be able to cope or perform his duty as at when due, the negligence of your duty will lead to queries which may further lead to a termination of your appointment or employment.

This is exactly what goes on in the corporate world, a lot of people lost their job because they are not disciplined.

When you are expected to resume work by 8.am in the morning, yet found wanting, always coming late to work by an hour after your resumption time, if it happens too often, you will definitely have problems with your employer. A friend of mine named Joseph got employment in a very big company with great pay, this guy was fortunate because as at that time there was few job, there were lots of graduates who have been in the labor market looking forward to secure a job. Joseph got the job, but he had a problem, he is used to coming late to work. Although, he was hard working, but just couldn't discipline himself to come early to work. The company only tolerated him for the fact that he was very resourceful, an unfortunate thing happened, the board of directors were going to have meeting one certain Monday morning and Joseph was in custody of vital documents which was to be discussed at the meeting and top of the agenda, despite getting a firsthand information for more than a week, on the day of the meeting, Joseph came an hour late to the meeting, he scrambled into the conference room, the venue of the meeting, everyone stared at him, Joseph became stupefied, at that moment it dawn on him that he had bitten more than he can chew.

The board of directors and management were so embarrassed; it took them another forty five minutes to wait after Joseph's late arrival for Joseph to locate the file. Immediately the meeting ended, Joseph was recommended for sack by the human resource manager and that was how he lost his job. That brings us to one of the major of factor that you need to know when it comes to discipline and that is punctuality.

Punctuality a Necessity

Punctuality is one of the major element of being disciplined, every area of life that has to do with meeting an appointment, attending a program either religious or non religious, coming early to work, going early to class, attending a practice or training session has everything to do with punctuality.

Punctuality therefore, is something that has to do with every person as long as you are a human being. As a child is born it is very necessary or essential to teach at early stage of the child's life self discipline, self discipline will help the effective development of the child. If you come late to programs you will end up not knowing what transpired there, same also it is when you are schedule to attend a religious service; you will miss out on a very important aspect of it. Now take example from the popular adage which says "the man who was not present at the funeral will start from the legs if asked to exhume the corpse".

Avoid Lateness

Self discipline is effective if you always strive to avoid lateness, whatever event you are participating in, always try to avoid lateness. Because lateness will not make people to take you serious, if you are known for coming late to programs, you will end up missing out on leadership positions or you will not be given responsibilities.

Take for instance, you may one day be given the responsibility of giving a speech in an organization or gathering, and when the audience are already seated waiting for you to give your speech, there is sudden announcement that you are yet to arrive, people will begin to view your absence as a habit that is akin to you.

Avoid Scandal

Self discipline will help you to avoid scandal; you will observe around the world that scandal is what is normally associated with the downfall of famous people. For instance, it is a common knowledge how some footballers or celebrities are accused of sexual abuses and rape cases, drug related offences, match fixing and tax evasion just to mention a few, these are issues that can send you to jail, and that can end an illustrious career. Self discipline therefore is very essential when it comes to being mentally tough; most people who are very tough are actually disciplined. If they are not disciplined, they will not get some level of success and they may end up having too many distraction that will affect their career.

People or candidates who are highly disciplined are in high demand in the labor market and in business organizations. If you are well disciplined you will always maintain a different level because a disciplined person will always exhibit some quality which may not be common. For instance, if you employ two candidates, and you discovered that one is very punctual, he comes to work early and resumes, he or she performs his duty with little or minimum supervision, the candidate takes his job as a major priority, he does his job neatly with dexterity such an individual is outstanding because he or she has a better approach to his job and a higher mental strength than someone who is always acting on the contrary by showing signs of lateness to work, not doing the job well, always prone to making mistakes, leaves his jobs uncompleted and always having not well finished product.

Self disciplined individuals are in high demand all over the world, such people bring high quality to the work place and their contributions always make the company to recognize them and give them awards, also they always stand out and make the company to feel they are indispensable. The company always feels threatened and fear they will lose client or the business of the company may be negatively affected by their departure. Hence, companies always try hard to make sure their important staffs are not leaving the employment. Such individuals also normally have long years of experience which help to train or raise other incoming young staff that will follow their lead.

Therefore, the company usually tries to keep them by giving out incentive, loans, and promotions and better pay rise that entice them or encourage them to stay with the company. What do you think is the reason why these individuals are able to get such or be in that level? It's simply because of their self discipline which they have maintained all the years. It takes someone with self discipline to also be able to get that kind of mental toughness and experience to get special recognition and getting that leadership role.

Self Discipline leads to leadership

Being a leader comes with great responsibility as long as human beings are concerned, anyone who is well disciplined will always attract some responsibilities and such responsibilities can be associated with leadership position. If you are well disciplined and you always perform your duties very well, someday, you may be given a leadership position, it may not be immediate, but someone is watching and evaluating your performance and it's only a matter of time.

The demand for success is always high in the corporate world, see everything that you do as a responsibility, no matter what is given to you, even if it's small task, make it very big by becoming successful with it.

Self discipline and will power on demand is what makes the corporate world very competitive, because in corporate organization the secret of major success recorded takes place when there are lots of people who are well discipline and are ready to take the organization to the next level. This usually comes with the various individual performances that is always felt in the business organization.

Chapter 5

Mindset

One of the most important factors that propels or determines the mental toughness of an individual is mindset. Whatever the mind can conceive it can achieve. This is a basic principle that has a worldwide or universal definition and lots of people talk about mindset a lot. The question now is what is your mindset? What do you understand by mind setting. First of all, your mindset determines what you believe in and what you think can be done or cannot be done. For instance, if you believe that something can be achieved, you will discover that someone else may not believe in what you think can be done. Hence, both of you have two different mindset.

There are different kinds of mindset, we have the positive mindset, and we also have the negative mindset. These two are different and we have different people with different mindset about something that is the subject of discussion. Have you notice at some point while you discussing certain issues with a friend or someone close to you, the person will tell you that it is not possible? The person said so because he or she doesn't believe what you think is possible and so he develops a different mindset towards what you have just said to him. In this life, everybody will not agree with you, but the ones who believe what you are telling actually share your views too.

I shall now show you the power of the different types of mindset that we have and also how you can decide to chose the right mindset. This is a very important aspect of our discussion, so I would like you to pay attention in the section. Mindset is one of the things that has help and also destroyed a lot of people. If you have a negative mindset, it will derail you, it will make you not to see what opportunities lie in front of you, I will expatiate further viz-a-viz:

Negative Mindset

Negative mindset occurs when a person decides to be adamant about something; the person's mindset is not adaptable to change in opinion or receptive to positive ideas and is not open to progressive initiatives. A negative mindset is stubbornly refusing to believe or participate or see what is obtainable in a particular venture or situation. Hence, negative mindset is actually the exact contrary of mental toughness, because the person who has a negative mindset will never shift his position when he is asked to do so in respect of a particular issue. People with negative mindset are not always open to opportunities.

The disadvantages of having a negative mindset

Those who have negative mindset are always limited in their achievement in nature, they are often average and will never think or accept any opportunity that will change their lives.

I have a friend of mine, we use to play together and we have been friends for over fifteen years. I got an opportunity to join a network marketing company which had a great compensation plan. I joined the company because I was able to see the opportunity of making a fortune and changing my life, so I decided to share the same opportunity with my friend, I invited him to come over and see the same opportunity that I saw.

To my greatest surprise, my friend wasn't interested despite the fact that I went as far as showing him my bank account balance; he saw how much I got as payment from the company. He just didn't care and he stayed passive and never joined me in the business. Therefore, people with negative mindset will never go far in life because they are not easily adaptable to change, they are always very stiff and not flexible in terms of forming positive opinion about something. Never be a person with a negative mindset because negative mindset is actually a negative mind, it will make you to be someone who is not ready to accept change and change is the only thing that is constant. Secondly, people who have a negative mindset are always having the negative opinion about something and they are usually mentally weak.

Inability to recognize opportunity

A negative mindset individual will never see opportunity when it comes. Opportunities comes once in a while and not every time, therefore for a person with negative mindset, it is several missed opportunity which repeatedly occurs for them. This is not good for mental development.

Passing over opportunities repeatedly

People with negative mindset will never have a high level of mental toughness because they have already made up their mind about something. They have concluded that they aren't going to participate or do whatever you tell them because they are not interested in the opportunity you are giving them. If the opportunity that comes their way is what will make a positive change in their lives, they will not listen and they will not see it and such negative thinking can lead to poverty. Hence, when we talk about being poor, we are talking of people who pass over opportunities repeatedly and that is exactly what people who are forming negative mindset always find themselves being at the end of the day, but no matter what opportunity is presented before them, they will never be open minded to it.

How Negative Mindset affects an Individual Mental Toughness

People with negative mindset generally lack mental toughness because of their numerous excuses, they always find a way of giving excuses and have explanations on why something cannot be done or achieved, unknowingly they don't always realize their mistakes. Sometimes they are so convinced and that situation doesn't and can't make them mentally tough.

Negative Mindset leads to procrastination

If you have a negative mindset, you will always have the tendency to procrastinate what you ought to do on time, this occurs when you are given a responsibility or task, you will just find yourself shifting and postponing what you ought to do at the right time till another time thereby leaving the job undone.

If you find yourself in this kind of situation, know that you have a mental weakness and you need to improve and get mentally tough. Example where people get mental weakness is when they leave their house untidy for months, anybody who fails or neglect doing his or her assignment without genuine reason is mentally weak, inability to keep appointments, being forgetful of important events or activities that you need to participate in, always coming late to meetings, missing lectures and examinations, unable to attend an interview, arriving late to important meetings, unable to be faithful to commitments such as marriage and relationship etc. these are some of the avenues where lack of mental toughness will always expose your mental weakness because you need to be mentally tough when you find yourself in the above mentioned relationship and daily activities.

Having a Positive Mindset

This part deals with people who have mental toughness. If you really want to be mentally tough, you have to fall into this category of people, you need to have a positive mindset. People who have positive mindset have the probability of being successful, most of the successful people in the world today are people who have positive mindset and they are often mentally tough.

Believing in yourself

When you have a positive mindset you will believe in yourself, you will also believe that you can make it. You have the ability to achieve anything, people who are successful in the world always believe in themselves, they have one thing in their mind and that is positivism which makes them to consistently work towards achieving their goals and from my experience, people who have positive mindset always achieve great things when they consistently do what they are doing consistently without relenting or showing complacency.

A positive minded person is mentally tough because when he or she embarks on a journey they don't look back until they have achieved what they want to achieve, arriving at their destination in a short time is what always occupy their thoughts and minds. These categories of people are always mentally tough and are always filled with the desire to do anything possible to get what they want.

Goal setting

If you want to be mentally tough, make sure you set goals for yourself, the goals you set will make you to always work towards achieving such goals. Goal setting is very essential, because it will enable you to continue to stay focused on the project that you are handling and not only when you are handling a project, but generally your mindset will become more focused and distinctively tailored towards being stronger and stronger, the strength of your mentality will increase and you will become mentally tough as long as you set goals for yourself. To set your goals you start by doing the following:

Write Down Your Goals

When you write down your goals, you will be able to determine what and when you want to achieve, this brings your mind to focus on those goals and also you will be able to work out a plan. In this circumstances your mind is constantly put into thinking about your goals every day, it causes and arouses mental activity in your head and the more you keep thinking about it, the chances of you keep working at achieving the goals. Remember, great people in the world today start by goal setting, and they keep dreaming about their goals and start activities that will enable them to achieve the goals.

If you are desirous of being mentally tough, you need to start developing a positive mindset by starting activities that will make you think and use your mental power by setting positive goals for yourself that will make you succeed.

Generally, when you have develop a positive mindset towards life, everything you do will be action oriented and you will have the conviction that anything is possible, *with such positive mindset, you will become mentally tough* and you will not settle for less. Being mentally positive is what differentiate people around the world, it is one of the characteristics that makes people very tough and as long as this is the case, we will always have successful people and unsuccessful people.

What you should do:

- Always have a positive mindset

- Believe anything is possible

- Don't entertain fear in your activity

- Your thinking should be positive

- Avoid friends who always have negative mindset

- Be friends with people who have positive mindset

- Study the people with positive mindset and try to do what they are doing to achieve success

- Study successful people and their routine

Chapter 6

Mental State

A mental state is a condition which defines a person's mental situation in a particular moment it has a relationship that has to do with a person's attitude, it represents a person perception at a particular point in time. There are various state of minds at a particular time, a person's mental state therefore can be any of the following: viz-a-viz:- love, pleasure, hate, pain and the attitudes flinging towards the proposition of believing, being afraid, conceiving something and hoping etc.

The state of your mind should not be something that will totally take over your mind to the extent that you refuse to accept the truth about a situation. Sometimes when we have the state of mind that has to do with love, something can change that state of mind and that is when a person suffers a heart break. Heart breaks therefore changes the positive perception and can make a person who suffers heart break to lament or feel regrets about the broken relationship. Your mental state therefore has the ability of bringing down your level of mental toughness even if you are mentally tough.

For example I'll like to share the mistake done by some people in the time of old. Samson was mentally tough as we knew about his mental state in the bible, he was powerful and was feared greatly, but he fell in love with a woman and he actually made a mistake by giving out the secrete of the source of his powers, here you can see how your mental state can affect your mental toughness. There are certain situations that will tend to cripple your mental state. The "mental state of love" is one of them, when you are competing, you need to remain focus on winning and you will need to concentrate, when you lost concentration you may be punished or miss the winning formula and that can become very costly simply because you shifted your mind and fell in love with something not connected to what you are doing.

For example, many great football teams in the world who have the potential of winning a competition often lost concentration and they end up being beaten. This is also a state of mind, when you lost concentration it is a sign that at that moment you have sustained mental weakness, instead of being tough you become weak.

Love and Concentration

Love is one mental state factor that can either make you to be mentally tough or mentally weak depending on the circumstance. If you are an athlete or you find yourself in any profession, in order for you to be mentally tough you must be able to love what you are doing. If you don't love what you are doing, then you don't need to be doing what you are doing. Because you will never become mentally tough, if you look around the world today we have great people, celebrities, athletes, great motivational speakers, great medical doctors, lawyers, engineers and scientist etc these people are successful and are mentally tough simply because they love what they are doing, they love their profession. So, whatever you are doing always make sure you love what you are doing, that is the first thing you need to become mentally tough.

How Love can affect you negatively

Now I'll like to talk about love, the type that can destroy your mental toughness, I've seen some great super stars who have been successful with the love they have for their profession, but as their career progressed they drifted and began to fall in love with what can destroy their body system, and that started to take a toll on their career. For example, taking alcohol and drugs as an athlete. If you are an athlete, there are certain substances that you don't need during the period of your career advancement and that is taking drugs and drinking heavy alcohol. Famous super stars have taken to drinking and when they are being discovered, it becomes a subject of public discussion. The media will always beam their search lights on the star, they are interested in knowing what they are doing, and they will always publish the negative parts or things that a super star is doing.

The clubs will not want their names to be dragged into any scandal because it will bring down their reputation and affect their rating and market value. So, you can see how loving circumstances can negatively affect the career of a person. Therefore, it is very important that you love the things that will help your career to progress positively. This will also enable you to develop mental toughness when your career gets a positive lift and better placed to become more successful.

Points to note

- Avoid falling in love with alcohol

- Avoid drug enhancement performance substances

- Don't keep or being around friends who love taking alcohol and drugs

- Stay away from anything that has bad influence on you

- Love your career or whatever you are doing

- Keep friends who are like minds and who want to be successful

- If you want to fall in love with someone, be sure the person loves you too, and per adventure you experience a break up, don't allow that to affect your mental state

- Don't cry over disappointment, just move on with your life

Hatred and Mental Toughness

There is something about you, things happen to you while you hate, you may decide to hate someone, but in actual fact, the person might not even know that you hate him or her. But I'll want you to know that, the more you hate, the more you get affected negatively and this leads to low mental toughness, because when you hate, you are the one suffering.

The person that you hate may be sitting in the same house, office, school or hall with you, while a lecture is going on, you'll discover that your mind may not be in the lecture, you may be thinking about that person that you hate, simply because you hate and don't want to see the person. In the end, you may not even gain anything from the lecture.

You may also hate your neighbor, and anytime you see him or her you just don't want to talk to him, all these emotions pile up and make you to put pressure on yourself and that will affect your blood pressure. You don't need it, so do not hate instead learn to show love, forgive and forget whatever happened or transpired between you and your neighbor and free yourself from the shackles of hatred.

If you refuse to stay away from hatred, you may end up committing a crime, because most times we have seen hate crimes committed against people who never knew that they have someone who hates them. When this happen the law enforcement agents will investigate and prosecute offenders and that means there is always a risk of going to jail.

When you go to jail, your condition begins to deteriorate because your mental toughness will be brought to a very low level where you begin to think and see yourself as a looser.

What to do:

- Don't hate show love instead
- Don't fight or quarrel with your neighbor
- Learn to say am sorry
- Forgive and forget
- Stay away from negativity
- Don't get jealous about your friend's achievement always wait for your own time which will always come

Pleasure and Mental toughness

Pleasure is doing something that your really enjoy doing such as always having the tendency to have fun. Pleasure therefore can also affect your mental toughness when you lack the control over enjoyment. If you are the type that is always enjoying something that gives you pleasure you will have problems in the future. Most pleasure that affect people negatively are the ones that they enjoy in excess. For instance if you are a sports person or an athlete and you love having sex, if this gets into your head, you will begin to lose focus on your main goals and you will find yourself chasing every woman that you see around you. Pleasure therefore is something that can hurt, instead focus on the things that will help build your mental strength and you will find yourself becoming very tough, for instance, if you are an amateur, you can work hard and find pleasure in training, take it as your fate and try as much as possible to enjoy every bit of the training. It will help in going a long way to affect your career positively.

Let me talk about one superstar that I find very amazing but later lost it because of pleasure. The story of brazil's legendary footballer is a perfect example of a super star with mesmerizing skill, he is a world class footballer who has won the FIFA world cup and many other trophies for club and country. If you watch him in training he always laughs and he is always full of smiles and he enjoys playing football, he practices with interest and he finds every skill pleasurable, to him while others struggled to gain mastery of ball control, he doesn't struggle, he just enjoy every bit of the ball in his possession and he is one of the great footballers that left his trade mark as a master trickster when it comes to dribble and ball control. This helped him a lot in his career, but he began to have problems when he began to have pleasure in drinking and night clubbing. This is a perfect example when pleasure takes over your mindset and you will tend to miss the major focus in your career. Mental toughness cannot be achieved when you enjoy things outside your field or career and this is not good for your development.

What you should do

- Find pleasure in learning

- Find pleasure in training

- Be interested in your career more than any other pleasure

- Enjoy what you are doing in respect of your career

- Stay away from pleasures that tend to make you lost focus on your goals

Pain and Mental Toughness

Pain is when you experience some form of difficulty, suffering and distress. Sometimes you want to give up on what you are facing in life; you just tell yourself "I can't take it anymore". This is what pain brings to you, making you feel the whole world is crashing on you. However, I'll like to guide you on the subject "pain". Pain can be very useful sometimes and pain can also discourage someone. But the truth of the matter is, it depends on what form of pain in perspective. Sometimes as a young student, apprentice or business man or woman, pain is necessary for you to be able to learn a lesson about your career.

If you've gone through life without a pain from anywhere, then you will not really understand what life is all about. "Life is not a bed of roses", when you experience easy life for many years, you may end up having a great hurt when pain comes your way. Now, pain is useful if it is coming from a training ground, if you are a soldier, you want to represent your country for instance, you want to join the military and fight in defending your country, you will need to undergo some special training to make you tough and fearless in facing any enemy that will attack your country. This is where painful training is very good. If you want to succeed in business, just like other successful business men and women, you may get your fingers burnt while you try so many businesses before you settle down for the right one that is perfect for profit maximization, all these are pain you need to go through so that you can succeed, if you are a student, when you are studying and reading hard, you need to attend lectures, you need to prepare for test and examinations by reading late in the night. These are the things that will make you to develop mentally and that is what makes you mentally tough, but if you fail to participate in lectures, you miss classes, you don't read for test and examination, hey! You are toiling with your education and may end up becoming a failure.

Therefore pain is necessary for our mental toughness, most celebrities and great athletes in the world today had to go through a lot of painful training and to be able to get to the level they are, and they did not have any other option than painful training. Sometimes they get hurt and injured in training and may be nursing injury for months and after the treatment, they still come back to continue where they have stopped, hence, this is a very good example of pain that is good for mental toughness. Remember "no pain, no gain!"

When Pain is caused by Defeat

Sometimes when you go through pain as a result of defeat, either you have worked so hard, to win a competition, you have studied so hard to pass an examination, you have been working on a project and you wanted to deliver a great project and despite all your efforts, it just didn't work out fine or the way you expected and you missed it. This can be very painful and may have the tendency of weakening you, making you to feel defeated and wanting to give up on your pursuit of success. If you give up, you have just calculated on how to become mentally weak. Here is what you should do, when you go through such or similar experience all you need to do is dust yourself up and get back on track.

Perhaps, there is something you didn't do that others did to succeed, find out that thing and go back to the drawing board and re-lunch yourself back to get what you want. It happens to most successful people and you can imagine if they didn't go back to sharpen their skill, they'll never be able to get to the top. This is one lesson that you need to learn, despite the fact that pain is good for training, when you experience disappointments, it can also cause you pain, the advise here is for you not to give up on your dreams.

If you want to be mentally tough, accept the pain and build your mental toughness painfully and you will gain a lot.

Key Points to do:

- Practice regularly
- Love painful training
- Build your mental strength through painful practice
- Accept pain and love it
- Relax and do the training
- Love the work hard type of training
- Don't get disappointed over missed opportunity
- Evaluate your performances and try again
- Work harder next time you take on challenges

Being Afraid as it Affects Mental Toughness

Mental toughness is not for people who are always afraid to try, anyone who really wants something should go for it, but the moment you begin to exercise doubt if that thing will work out or not, that is just the beginning of your downfall. Always make serious efforts to become mentally tough by not being afraid to try new things. The story of the owner of Kentucky Fried Chicken (KFC) is amazing. He was already old, at the age of over 65, this man thought of trying out something in order to start earning a living, after being out of service, he had nothing left.

He still needed some money to continue to live the rest of his life, he thought about preparing chicken source and selling it from door to door, today the rest is history, Kentucky Fried Chicken is a house old name and is present in many countries around the world. If the owner did not conceive the idea, if he did not dare to try, how would he make that great impact and great success? Don't be afraid of what you think you can do to succeed, being afraid will only limit your potentials.

Conceiving Something and Hoping

When you begin to conceive something and hoping to get that thing, it will just be there like an idea, which needs to be brought to life. Mental toughness is not meant to be in isolation. You need to conceive as well make it happen. You may have a great idea, but until you begin to design the way that idea is going to manifest from you, it stays where you are keeping it. Just like when you place something in a cooler, it will remain in the cooler until you orchestrate it to operate.

Chapter 7

Develop an Unbeatable Mind

To become mentally tough you need to develop an unbeatable mind, the mind that always says to himself or herself, I'm the greatest and I can achieve anything and nothing can stop me. That is an unbeatable mind. Many people in the world today have problems with their jobs, career, business, education and projects, simply because they lack the unbeatable mind. Let me share from experience one man who constantly claimed to be the greatest, when he started and when he usually make such bold claim "I am the greatest!" people thought that he was joking, but he eventually was, as many years passed, his track records in the world boxing is still a point of reference. He is no other than the late "Mohammed Ali". He had such a mindset that stubbornly claimed that he was the greatest, he was able to defeat so many opponents and even the ones he lost to, he came back to beat them.

The unbeatable mindset doesn't believe that someone can beat him or her, an unbeatable mindset always and constantly makes bold claim statement by being convinced that nothing can stop him or hold him back, when you get to that level you will definitely be mentally tough and actually nothing will pull you down. These are some of the characteristics of someone with an unbeatable mindset which you should know and begin to put in practice:

Fearless and Mentally Tough

What is the meaning of fear? Fear is when you are afraid of something, either object or abstract. Some philosophy say that "FEAR" means "Falls Evidence Appearing Real". When you have the fear that something negative is going to happen to you, it might be so, because you just believed and you are convinced within your heart that something negative is going to happen to you. When you have this constant fear, you can never be mentally tough. Let me show you an example of one man in the scriptures who was always afraid that he might lose all his riches.

He is Job, the bible tells of his story as one man who feared God and was greatly rich, but there was one thing about job, he always had the fear that he might lost all his riches someday and he did, and what did he had to say? He said "that which I feared most has finally befallen me"

You see how being afraid can bring about the opposite of mental toughness. If you are a person who is always filled with fear of something, it's time to change and have an unbeatable mindset. Don't always conceive in your mind that something negative is going to happen to you, rather be convinced that something positive is going to happen to you. That is one of the ways to develop and unbeatable mindset.

"Yes I can" - Unbeatable Mindset"

There are many people in the world today who have difficulty in telling themselves that they can do something. Majority of these category of people are not always achieving anything in life because they never have the conviction that they can do what other people who are successful are doing to get to the top. Once you are unable to have the constant conviction that "yes I can" you'll be where you are until you begin to believe you actually can do something.

I have been in position where I sampled out a lot of people, and there was a particular thing I needed to be done for me, as I went round looking for someone to help me out, majority of the people I came across were always telling me "no I can't do it" am not talking about doing something negative, no! It was a simple task that needed to be done. But surprisingly only one boy who was about 15 years old accepted to do it and he did what even a 25 year old said he couldn't do. You see, that's the problem with many people in the world today, they just don't believe that they can do something. Whether it is, in business, education, career, sports and other areas of human endeavors, they aren't just bold enough to have that mentality of "yes I can". The unbeatable mindset will not be complete without accepting and believing in the "yes I can".

I want to tell you today that "yes you can", I want to let you know that you can make it to the top, I want to tell today that I believe anyone can rise and get to the pinnacle of his or her career, but if I say "yes you can" and you refuse to say "yes I can" there is nothing anyone can do about it, because you've not gotten that conviction. So, I need you to say it to yourself as many times as possible "yes I can", say it every ten minutes and every time and you will see the impact. There you go; you will begin to develop an unbeatable mindset.

Use what you have to your advantage

For you to have an unbeatable mindset there is something important I'll like to let you know and that is, using what you have at a greater advantage to achieve what you want. You are a unique person and there are no two persons other than you and there are no other you but you. What this means is that everyone has a talent and that can be used to a great advantage against any opponent or contemporary. Therefore use it to your advantage, if you refuse to use your talent or what you have better, someone else will use his or hers to better advance. So you have to find a way to succeed in the survival of the fittest and one of the finest ways to become mentally tough is by having unbeatable mindset, to use what you have as an advantage to your own benefit. Christiano Ronaldo, Lionel Messi, Michael Jordan, Magic Johnson, Late Michael Jackson, Late Michael Faraday etc. all these great people did not just exist without using their talent to a great advantage.

They started by discovering their talents and they began to develop it by constantly using it and making it becoming relevant and they did that every day and today they have successfully stamp their history and authority in the sands of time. Michael Jackson was discovered alongside his brothers, he was gifted, he had a special kind of talent, which included his ability to sing, dance and also drew a lot of attention from audience. When he discovered himself he began to practice and he had a different kind of personality which was as a result of developing unbeatable mindset. He stayed on top of his game and he won so many awards, broke so many records. So to have an unbeatable mindset, use everything that you have got, your talent and your biggest advantage is when you are able to make use of what you have got.

Remember the parable of the talents, each of them were given different talents of different values, some use their talents and multiplied, and they receive more rewards and praises by their masters, some went to hide theirs, and even the little they had was taken away from them and given to someone who had more. That is a very big lesson that you have to learn about life, always make use of what you have got. Don't abandon your talent and start looking for result somewhere else. The answer to your desires lies within you, seek it, find it and use it.

Constant Practice

To have an unbeatable mindset, you have to engage yourself in constant practice of what you know how to do. You are the only one who know how you do your thing and you are the best at what you do, you are not the best at what someone else does for you, No! You are the best at what you are doing for yourself presently. This is the basis of what it takes to developing an unbeatable mindset; don't think someone else will make you to be the best. Only teachers, coaches and trainers will show you the basics and technical part of what you need to know, but you still have to do it yourself in other to discover your abilities.

Constant practice can only be achieved when you are ready or prepare your mind to get into it. Don't always act as if someone is forcing you to do something, let your mind be made up that this is what you want and it is possible only if I involve myself in constant practice.

Constant practice therefore makes the job easier and your gaining mastery and perfection can only be achieved when you continue to work on something continuously. It may take some time to achieve, it may not be easy in the first instance, but it's definitely worth it when you start, don't look back and make sure you put the right facilities that will help you succeed. For instance, you want to start a career in football, you don't need a ping pong ball, you need a football, you need to play basket ball, what you need is basketball and a basketball court where you can practice etc.

Again talent may not be enough, but constant practice will go a long way to further develop your talent, if you want to be the best, you need to develop your talent through constant practice. I have seen superstars in football learn and practice how to take free kicks, for instance, David Beckham, one of the English footballers was a free kick specialist, I've seen him take three free kicks in a match and he scored all three. It couldn't have been possible without constant practice. Hence, constant practice is the key to developing unbeatable mindset because he believed in his ability to score free kicks even from long range and it was so for him.

Whatever you need, whatever you want to achieve, you need to get into practice of that thing from the armature level and move on to the professional which is your next level.

Be Excited
You really want to make it to the top, you have to be very excited, developing a mindset is not when you are sad or

neutral, if you are not excited about what you are doing or feeling too much pressure you may not get what you want. Hence, I'll advise that you stay excited, always see that there is something great coming out of what you are doing. Excitement brings out the best in you, because your level of adrenalin will always be high. When you know the potential and chances behind what you are doing, you will always feel the need to always get things done to a level that you will become satisfied. The move, the plan and everything that you are doing must involve excitement, without excitement you will not stay afresh. Excitement makes you look fresh, putting a smile on your face will make you feel good, simply because you are excited about what you are doing, again excitement brings the feeling of goodness, being pleased with yourself when you discovered that you are making progress before the competition starts or during preparation for an event makes it possible for you to build up an unbeatable mindset. Excitement doesn't bring discouragement, when you are excited you will always be encouraged to do more and become successful at what you are doing. Today, I encourage you to be excited no matter what you are going through and you will be prepared to face the biggest challenge and defeat it.

Whenever you discover that you are down or discouraged, try to raise your excitement level, because that is just the tonic you need. Feeling disappointed about something that didn't go as you expected is a common phenomenon that most people go through. But when it happens to you, don't feel bad about it; all you need to do is raise your excitement level. Look into the future and see yourself already where you want to be, smile and laugh at any disappointment, feel happy that you have already won the battle, don't let disappointments bring you down, and you will be glad that you are always feeling excited about your project or career.

Chapter 8

Iron Will

Your will is your disposition or inclination towards something, but when you have an "iron will", it means an unbending disposition that tends to show that you insist on something and you are not ready to compromise. In mental toughness, you need to have an "iron will" because it will make you to be specific in what you want. Your desire for something can be tested by your willingness to carry out some activities that can make you achieve that thing. Therefore when we talk about having "iron will" we talk about that person who stays like a fortress and committed to the course of achieving that one thing that he or she desires so much.

To have an iron will you must have the following characteristics:-

Being Resolute

To be resolute means that you are unyielding, not unyielding to simple advise or instructions, No! it means that you are not ready to give up any of your desires to advance. Many people in the world today are not resolute, many always compromise with failure while some other persons will go all out to give what it takes to become successful in whatever endeavor that they embark on, you must be resolute always drawing between the lines where you want to go and where you do not want to go.

You have to be unbendable if you really want to be the best, unbendable to defeat, even if you have suffered defeat do not yield to it, by staying down, no! You keep moving, when you fall, rise and walk whatever it takes make sure you do not yield to defeat, this will make you have a very strong and powerful will that will further increase your mental toughness.

Don't Accept Excuses

Many people in the world today always find a way of having an excuse or reason for failure. They'll always want people to sympathize with them; this is a sign of mental weakness. I used to say to myself, I owe no one any explanation for failure or success. I'll not yield to any excuses, if you have a reason why you need to be successful, then, you will not entertain excuses. Giving excuses so many times will never make you to become serious at anything, the more excuses you give, the more you will have unfinished jobs and it will never stop. Don't allow excuses to become part of you, excuses is like a character, once you allow it to become part of you, it will become obvious that many people will begin to notice your excuses.

Excuses is not the best option when it comes to being mentally tough, so you need to avoid all forms of excuses which will never contribute successfully to your mental development. Giving too many excuses will make you look irresponsible, it breeds procrastination and what you ought to have finished on time will be delayed for another session, which is the ugly side of having too many excuses. You want to have the mindset of someone who is desirous of not being yielding or being influenced, then you need to become more accustomed to avoiding excuses. Don't give excuses when there is no time to carry out a task. Make sure you desire what you want and also give people the opportunity to know what is really going on. Which means that you should let people know you as somebody who doesn't give excuses in other to carry out his or her responsibilities.

Having Genuine Integrity

When we are talking about iron will, it doesn't have to do with your mind alone; there is a particular trend about having iron will which has to do with your kind of person too. When you are known for something positive, something that everyone around you who knows you and can always talk or able to say something about your kind of person, that means your iron will has been able to affect others positively. You must learn to have a genuine integrity, not all integrity are genuine, integrity means that you have uprightness, when I am talking about being upright, I don't refer to people who show their uprightness by way of eye service, No! I'm talking the one that people can say something positive about you genuinely even in your absence, therefore, it is very essential to talk about having genuine integrity.

People will always remember you for something that you are known for and one of those things that represent your iron will is integrity. Integrity is something that enables people to understand and know that this man can be someone we can rely on or we can entrust him for something maybe money, position or anything that has to do with leadership. Whatever you are doing always try as much as you can to have that integrity because integrity is one of the features that makes you different and it will boost your mental toughness not only for yourself alone, but also you become an influential person.

Be Honest

Being truthful about your opinion and in whatever you say and in whatever you are doing goes a long way to tell about your kind of person, if you are not honest when you are entrusted with something important, then the chances is that people will no longer see you as a honest person. Always make sure that whenever you are in a position or entrusted with something, make sure you are always honest. Even if you are not given any office or particular responsibility, it is your responsibility to be an honest person. If you are not honest, then it will be very difficult for you to develop iron will within yourself. Iron will is one of the characteristics of a person who has mental toughness and if you really want to aspire to be tough then you must live a honest life.

Be flexible by Practical

Sometimes if you are strict, you will miss the point when it comes to human relationship, being strict is good but at the same time it can be counterproductive, you need to be very diplomatic in your relationship with people, that means you have to study people and understand them, secondly you have to be flexible in other to accommodate others because everyone cannot be on the same page. For instance if you have a particular ideology, such as being a republican for example, not everyone is a republican like you, others can be democrats or communist and when they air their views, it may be quite different from your own views, hence, you need to know how to relate with people in that circumstances. This means that you will need to be flexible while others air their views, then you can give a sound judgment about issues, but if you fail to do so, it means you will not be able to maintain that iron will. Sometimes you may be right about some issues and sometimes you may be wrong about particular issues. So you need to be able to strike a balance between your own opinion and that of others.

Be Trustworthy

The mistake that most people make in life is their inability to be trusted, some people can be so difficult to trust because they have been tested before and they failed. Don't fall prey to this categorization of not being able to be trusted. Trust is an important aspect of human existence; if you cannot be trusted then it will be very difficult for you to have a smooth human relationship. Every business relationship require some level of trust, if you have a product in the market, people must be able to trust what you are offering them or else you will not record sales. Trust therefore, means that you are always worthy of people's believe and faith in you, and when people have given you their trust, don't betray it. If you do, your Iron will can be affected when people no longer see you as someone that is trustworthy. Remember, having iron will is not about you alone, it also involves the ability to affect other people's life and perception about you, if you cannot find yourself in this position, then your iron will is just yourself and you alone.

Chapter 8

Confidence

Confidence is when you have "self belief". You have the ability to make yourself mentally tough by having that confidence and you have the ability to make yourself irrelevant by not having confidence in yourself, so the ball is in your court.

Before you can say that you are confident, you have to be truthful about it. You can only be informed by your conscience, when you think and discern about being confident. Hence being confidence is more of a personal thing, if others have confidence in you, it means you have develop yourself and you have proven to them that you are confident and they also know that you are confident. But when you are being personal with confidence, it means you have the conviction that you are confident about yourself. Therefore, for you to be confident you must possession the following characteristics;

High Self Esteem

No what it takes, there is one thing that matters most when it comes to confidence and that is "low self esteem". Low self esteems is dangerous because it kills the spirit of a person who has it. It is also very important to know also that when you have low self esteem, people easily notice it and that can be used against you. Low self esteem tends to expose the weakness of a person who has it. For instance, if you are competing for a prize and your opponents realizes that you have low self esteem, you are in for serious trouble because, a clever opponent will start by using mind games against you, your opponents will try as much as they can to talk you down and make you crumble in the competition. Make sure you always maintain a high level of self esteem. Don't quit, don't think or form the opinion that you are not the best when it comes to competing with others, start realizing that you can make it and beat your chest and say to yourself "I'm confident am going to succeed!"

Self Believe in Fostering Confidence

There is nothing as solid as believing in yourself, and there is no way you can talk about self confidence without you believing in yourself. To be mentally tough you have to believe totally in yourself, you have to believe in your own abilities. If you do not believe in yourself, it means if someone else believes in you, you will let them down. You don't let people down by not believing in yourself, you give people inspiration and they will see you as a role model if you believe in yourself and become successful.

To believe in yourself, you need self conviction, talk to yourself every day, that you are good, talk to yourself everyday that you are the best, you owe no one apology for claiming to be the best, whenever you want to perform a task, say to yourself "I am the best" and you will drive your mindset towards that direction. As much as self confidence is important, many people lack it and that's why we have so many people who are average, even with the potential of advancing, they just don't want to move to the next level. It's all because of lack of confidence because they don't actually believe that they have a potential that can improve their lives.

Points to note:

- Avoid low self esteem

- Build up your confidence level

- Think greatness

- Don't think small

- Meditate on your life and think about advancement

- Contemplate on yourself and see through your inner self

- See yourself as someone that is about to explode

- Say to yourself, the world is waiting for my arrival everyday

Chapter 9

Achieve the Success

Successful people are always celebrated, success is like a light that cannot be hidden, whenever there is a success recorded somewhere, either in a competition, games, business, education, technological advancement, science, medicine, arts etc. there is always some form of awareness created either in any of the sector involved.

Like I have enumerated in this book, successful people have mental toughness. To achieve success you need to holistically put into practice what needs to be done and you will definitely achieve it. It is a combination of so many factors that leads to success. Majority of it depends on you. You can decide to achieve success and you can decide to chose where you want to belong.

To achieve success you need to begin immediately, and how do you get started? You will need to begin by doing the following:

Leave your Comfort Zone

Success is not usually achieved by continuing in your normal state or doing what you have been doing that is not making you to advance, no! Success cannot be achieved if you are not ready to do what successful people do to become successful. Hence, you need to adjust and adapt to a lot of changes. You need to work harder and begin to train like it was your last chance to become successful. Successful people usually go the extra mile, it means you have to cut what you eat, it means you have to reduce the number of time you spend at the club or the number of times you spend relaxing.

Maximize a better usage of your time by drawing up a program that will guide you in whatever you are doing, make sure you allocate every time you have in a day, week, months and year to some form of activity that will make you to become successful.

Take stock, fall back and review your activities and analyze areas that need improvements and where you need to step up.

Take action immediately, avoid procrastination and get things done promptly without being urged to do so. Make sure a day doesn't go without you achieving something that will bring you success. Be persistent about it.

When you have achieved success, make sure you manage it very well, because success can be achieved and can also be lost if not properly managed.

The champion is in you; bring it out by being mentally tough!

Chapter 10

Conclusion

Successful people are mentally tough, to be successful in life, you have to be well prepared mentally, whether it is in your family, business, work or education. You have to have some level of mental development to be able to handle objection, the good and bad side of life.

Mental toughness therefore is very relevant and important to every individual. The world population keeps increasing, so many challenges coming up on daily basis. So you get uncomfortable sometimes, because everything going around you tends to affect you, from politics, leadership, work, business, family etc. everyone seems to be involved and affected and then some things happen that affects you.

The truth you cannot deny and avoid is the fact that as long as we are all humans, everyone needs mental toughness. When the theory of survival of the fittest was propounded, other theories later emerged which postulates that some living things will have to struggle for their survival and it is those living things that were better adapted to changes in their environment that will be able to survive the changes in their environment. Therefore, you should know by now, that there will always be changes in our life and environment, the question is "how well will you be able to adapt to such changes?"

Secondly, ask yourself "have you developed that features that will enable you to carry out your own adaptation"?

Then it is very clear that one of the distinctive features you will need to develop is your level of mental toughness. Whether you like it or not, you need to develop yourself mentally and it will start somewhere, you may be scared right now on how to begin, let me tell you something, your waiting days are over, the simple truth now is that you have to get things started, taking actions is what you really need, and by the time you start with a single step that you decide to take now, you will sooner or later look back and see the distance you would have covered.

Don't wait any longer, take that bold step in the right direction, follow the basic principles and teachings as explained in this book, step by step and one at a time, always refer back to the contents and read to gain mastery of the various approaches and directives given in order to advance further.

The moment is now; get the right mentality to handle any situation you find yourself no matter what the circumstances. Be mentally tough and you will be victorious forever!